WUTHERING HEIGHTS

A Commentary

R.S. SHARMA
Professor, Department of English,
Banaras Hindu University

ATLANTIC
PUBLISHERS & DISTRIBUTORS (P) LTD

Published by

ATLANTIC

PUBLISHERS & DISTRIBUTORS (P) LTD

7/22, Ansari Road, Darya Ganj, New Delhi-110002
Phones : +91-11-40775252, 40775214, 23273880, 23275880
Fax: +91-11-23285873
Web: www.atlanticbooks.com
E-mail: orders@atlanticbooks.com

Printed & bound in India by Atlantic Print Services

Preface

I had initially promised a 10-15 page introduction to *Wuthering Heights*, but no sooner had I begun to write than the sinister spell was cast. The work, as I contemplated it, started vibrating like a sentient growing creature, putting forth new limbs, striking the mind's eye with unforeseen beauties and terrors. I became involved in such issues as the true nature of good and evil, the characters of Heathcliff and Catherine, the subtleties of Emily Brontë's narrative techniques, her poetic power and mystical experience, and her relation to the cultural and literary traditions of Europe. And then there were some well-known interpretations of *Wuthering Heights* to be closely looked at.

While engrossed in dealing with these things, I forgot the stipulated limit; and when I did stop by an effort of the will, it was too late; hence this little book. Still, I hope I have not unnecessarily included anything about the novel which is not worth saying or re-saying.

I believe this book will prove useful to the serious student of Emily's novel and also point to fresh avenues of interpretation and research to committed scholars.

I received valuable assistance from my colleague, Dr. (Miss) Asha Vishwas and my student, Seema Singh in checking and correcting the typescript. For this, I gladly express my thanks to them. If some genuine errors still remain, they are to be set down to my account.

R.S. SHARMA

CONTENTS

1. The Genii of the Place

Wuthering Heights is a product of the powerful imagination of a woman writer, Emily Brontë – one of the three gifted daughters of Patrick Brontë, an Irish Clergyman, who was in charge of the parsonage of Haworth in the West Riding of Yorkshire. Born in 1818 she spent nearly all her life in the locality of her home and developed a deep mystical affinity with the nature of the place: high land with low vegetation, steep rugged rocks and hills constantly harried by strong north wind. The community that lived there was untouched (but not without premonitions) by the growing culture of the Industrial Revolution. Emily's identification with the ambience of the place created in her mind a firm belief that the human personality is an extension of the forces of nature that played around it – and herein lies an important key to the novel.

Wuthering Heights, subject to a harsh treatment by nature, is productive of strongly marked eccentric humans: Mr. Earnshaw, Hindley and Catharine; and Thrushcross Grange situated in a small valley makes for milder, urbane and enervated people: Edgar Linton and Isabella. Mr. Earnshaw, who had gone to Liverpool for something else, suddenly decides to bring a gipsy foundling home; he calls him after his lost son and begins to show undue partiality to him. Heathcliff himself, whose blood contains the elements of violent passion, fits the climate of Wuthering Heights like a glove and attracts Catherine like a powerful magnet. Their life together in the midst of heather and rock creates a bond which no power on earth can sunder, and yet, knowing this symbiotic dependence full well, Catherine rushes into marrying Edgar Linton. Hindley, when he takes a dislike to Heathcliff, goes to the extreme in humiliating and torturing him, and when he comes back from college, he brings a wife without any prior information; on the other hand the children of Thrushcross Grange are weak and pliable. Returning after an inexplicable absence of three years, when Heathcliff threatens the peace of Edgar's married life, the latter is nonplussed and has no courage to face his adversary or take effective action against his intrusions. His sister Isabella develops a fascination for Heathcliff and falls an easy prey to his calculated move.

2. The Two Principles

Critics have attributed a mystical import to this opposition: they find in it Emily's perception of the transcendental reality. In his detailed discussion of *Wuthering Heights*, David Cecil discerns the following elements of Emily Brontë's philosophy:

> The first is that the whole created cosmos, animate and inanimate, mental and physical alike, is the expression of certain living spiritual principles – on the one hand what may be called the principle of storm – of the harsh, the ruthless, the wild, the dynamic; and on the other the principle of calm – of the gentle, the merciful, the passive and the tame.
>
> Secondly, in spite of their apparent opposition these principles are not conflicting. Either – Emily Brontë does not make clear what she thinks – each is the expression of a different aspect of a single pervading spirit; or they are the component parts of a harmony. They may not seem so to us. The world of our experience is, on the face of it, full of discord. But that is only because in the cramped condition of their earthly incarnation these principles are diverted from following the course that their nature dictates, and get in each other's way.

If we pursue this line of thought in our reading of the novel, then a neat pattern seems to emerge. In the younger generation – that of Hareton and Cathy – the two principles begin to operate in unison; each is moderated by the other in the mixed composition of the two young people – Hareton's silly mother, Frances, it may be assumed, did not belong to the storm group. In the final chapters of the novel we see love in its earthly and gentle form making itself felt between the descendants of the two families, although not altogether without the Wuthering Heights tang. Mr. Lockwood, who in the beginning had seen the utter degradation of Cathy and Hareton, himself is a witness to a different scene:

> His handsome features glowed with pleasure, and his eyes kept impatiently wandering from the page to a small whitehand over his shoulder, which recalled him by a smart slap on the cheek whenever its owner detected such signs of inattention.

The novel ends with a firm note of happiness and hope when Lockwood declares that "they [Cathy and Hareton] are afraid of nothing" and that "together, they would brave satan and all his legion"; and also of peace after so much strife: "how anyone could ever imagine unquiet slumbers for the sleepers in that quiet earth." The spiritual message of *Wuthering Heights*, then, can be summed up in the language of a mystic:

> Sin is Behovely, but
> All shall be well, and
> All manner of thing shall be well.

Virginia Woolf, too, understandably, gathers the essence of the novel in cosmic terms, but her conclusion is different:

> She (Emily Brontë) looked out upon a world cleft into gigantic disorder and felt within her the power to unite it in a book. That gigantic ambition is to be felt throughout the novel – a struggle half thwarted but of superb conviction, to say something through the mouths of her characters which is not merely "I love" or "I hate", but "we the whole human race" and "you, the eternal powers...." the sentence remains unfinished.

Like Virginia Woolf, Elizabeth Drew is skeptical about the reconciliation of the two spiritual principles distinguished by David Cecil; according to her they represent two "separate planes of existence which remain disparate and irreconcilable in the world of men". This contention seems to gain strength from Hareton's decision to vacate Wuthering Heights and leave it in the possession of the spirits of Heathcliff and Catherine.

3. Genetic Blending

This philosophical interpretation is quite helpful, but it does not reveal the whole truth about the novel. We must descend from the metaphysical heights and explore the theme in terms of human stuff, almost in genetic terms. Now there is no doubt that Hareton and Cathy, in the course of the novel display much greater flexibility and accommodation than Heathcliff, Hindley and Edgar: they began with an acute antipathy towards each other and ended up by not only tolerating each other's quirks but by falling in love. In the final chapters we are given a glimpse of their life together which shows that they are now two fine specimens of human nature combining the two extreme types depicted in the novel in just the right proportion; neither too strong nor too weak, neither eccentric nor formless, neither violent nor passive. And they were so from the beginning, but their true nature was prevented from revealing itself owing to Heathcliff's ill-treatment.

The author is surely conveying the idea of an attractive blend of the two strains through Nelly's description of young Cathy's personality:

> She was the most winning thing that ever brought sunshine into a desolate house – a real beauty in face, with the Earnshaw's handsome dark eyes, but the Lintons' fair skin and small features, and yellow curling hair. Her spirit was high, though not rough, and qualified by a heart sensitive and lively to excess in its affections. That capacity for intense attachments reminded me of her mother; still she did not resemble her; for she could be soft and mild as a dove, and she had a gentle voice and pensive expression; her anger was never furious, her love never fierce – it was deep and tender.

4. The Mysteries

But this interpretation accounts for only one of the several transcendental elements in the novel. Another problem is the mystery of Heathcliff himself. Presenting the foundling to his wife Mr. Earnshaw says, "I was never so beaten with anything in my life; but you must e'en take it as a gift of God, though it's as dark as if it came from the Devil." It appears Mr. Earnshaw picked up the swarthy being under some superhuman compulsion: "I was never so beaten with anything in my life." The suffering Heathcliff brought with him was perhaps part of a greater purpose, or may be, he was indeed love in its pristine grandeur, which, diverted from its course by human weakness turned violent and destructive. Emily Brontë leading a life of isolation in bleak surroundings may have experienced the mystery of God's touch the way a Christian mystic does. Here is Hopkins, for example, groaning under the weight of Christ, the tiger:

> But ah, but O thou terrible, why wouldst thou rude on me
> Thy wring-world right foot rock? Lay a lionlimb
> against me? scan
> With darksome devouring eyes my bruised bones?

and more explicitly:

> Wert thou my enemy, O thou my friend,
> How wouldst thou worse, I wonder, than thou dost
> Defeat, thwart me.

If we concentrate on the name Heathcliff, we find that it contains two important features of the moorland with which Emily Brontë was in intimate relationship. She wrote in a poem:

> I'll walk where my own nature would be leading –
> It vexes me to choose another guide –
> Where the grey flocks in ferny glens are feeding,
> Where the wild wind blows on the mountainside.
>
> What have those lonely mountains worth revealing?
> More glory and more grief than I can tell:
> The earth that wakes one human heart to feeling
> Can centre both the worlds of Heaven and Hell.

This will lead us to the crux of Romanticism: the mystical oneness of nature and man. Emily Brontë appears to have keenly felt this oneness or correspondence. As her sister Charlotte observed she was "a native and nursling of the moors." And Catherine, her *alter ego*, too, is of the moors; they are her natural elements and she is in love with them. She is drawn to the gypsy boy because he is also of the moors; Heathcliff, as it were, is the incarnation of wild nature and his violent passion for Catherine is the passion of wild nature, which, like a torrent from the depths of the rock, when obstructed, turns fierce and pulls down everything coming in its way.

The love of Heathcliff and Catherine is the mating of the elements; it goes much deeper than sexual attraction; it is a mystical force of nature under whose action the two souls have fused together; try to separate them, and it is like cutting a single organism into two: each wriggling and suffering like the separated parts of an earthworm. Catherine cannot say how it is, but she knows what it is:

> My love for Heathcliff resembles the eternal rocks beneath – a source of little visible delight, but necessary. Nelly, I am Heathcliff! He's always, always in my mind – not as a pleasure, any more than I am always a pleasure to myself, but as my own being. So don't talk of our separation again; it is impracticable, and –"

This adamantine bond is the rock foundation of *Wuthering Heights*; it exists at once at the superhuman and sub-human levels and demolishes the barrier of death: death makes no difference to Heathcliff and Catherine – and to them only; to others, there may be ghosts. Every moment after her death, Heathcliff is in the agonising hope of meeting Catherine; he is keeping her room ready and would not allow anyone to lodge there. On hearing Lockwood's dream he is convinced that Catherine had called:

> "Come in! Come in! "he sobbed. "Cathy, do come. Oh do – once more! Oh! my heart's darling! hear me this time, Catherine, at last!"

No wonder, when this mighty base is fractured there is an earthquake in the affairs of the two houses involved, bringing torture and death for so many.

But even this holocaust has no power to remove Catherine from the scene. She is like Wordsworth's Lucy :

> No motion has she now, no force;
> She neither hears nor sees;
> Rolled round in earth's diurnal course,
> With rocks, and stones, and trees.

But with one important difference; she has both motion and force – quite a lot :

> I cannot look down to this floor, but her features are shaped on the flags! In every cloud in every tree – filling the air at night, and caught by glimpses in every object, by day I am surrounded with her image! The most ordinary faces of men, and women – my own features mock me with a resemblance. The entire world is a dreadful collection of memoranda that she did exist, and that I have lost her.

The final mystery we are confronted with is the change of heart in Heathcliff. Critics have often assigned this change to the exhaustion of his urge to destroy: his zest for revenge has spent itself. The following disclosure made to Nelly is quoted in support:

> An absurd termination to my violent exertions? I get levers and mattocks to demolish the two houses, and train myself to be capable of working like Hercules, and when everything is ready, and in my power, I find the will to lift a slate off either roof has vanished! My old enemies have not beaten me; now would be the precise time to revenge myself on their representatives – I could do it, and none

> could hinder me. But where is the use? I don't care for striking, I can't take the trouble to raise my hand! That sounds as if I had been labouring the whole time, only to exhibit a fine trait of magnanimity. It is far from being the case – I have lost the faculty of enjoying their destruction, and I am too idle to destroy for nothing.

One may, however, still ask: What caused this loss of the faculty to destroy? In our search for an answer, we are again led to a mystical phenomenon. In Chapter 29, when Heathcliff goes to Thrushcross Grange to fetch Cathy, now his daughter-in-law, home, he confides to Nelley that, the day before, he had opened Catherine's coffin. The sight of her body had a magical effect on him and he would have stayed there for ever, if the sexton had not stirred him. In that moment spiritualism and demonism became strangely indistinguishable and we can't say which is which. Has at last the ghost of Catherine, like the demon lover, possessed Heathcliff and will now drag him to his doom? He does, later, show the signs of a man possessed. Or has he had the rare mystical experience of spiritual reunion with Catherine. Heathcliff's own reaction points towards a favourable interpretation. Being admonished by Mrs. Dean for disturbing the dead, which is a very wicked deed, he replies:

> Disturbed her? No! she has disturbed me, night and day, through eighteen years – incessantly – remorselessly – till yesternight; and yesternight I was tranquil. I dreamt I was sleeping the last sleep by that sleeper, with my heart stopped and my cheek frozen against hers.

It is true that this event fails to stop the process of torture and brutality: that will continue for some more time; but the reason seems to be that the machinery of cruelty as well as the habit, had been strung so tight, that it would take time to become completely relaxed and neutralised. However, a sign of change is clearly perceptible. Within a fortnight of Lockwood's departure from Thrushcross Grange, Mrs. Dean was summoned to Wuthering Heights and she was quick to perceive an unexpected change in Heathcliff; he had begun avoiding any company and appeared to be already inhabiting another world. He seemed to be in an inner exultation, as if in wait for some mysterious bliss, so powerful in contemplation that he ceased to care for food and rest:

> Heathcliff stood at the open door; he was pale and he trembled; yet, certainly, he had a strange joyful glitter in his eyes that altered the aspect of his whole face.

He had earlier informed Mrs. Dean that he had lost the faculty of enjoying the destruction of Hareton and Cathy and that there was a strange change approaching; when asked what he meant by change, he replied in a truly mystical language:

> "I shall not know that, till it comes," he said; "I'm only half conscious of it now."

When the end came, it came peacefully, like that of a contented man, but his eyes wouldn't close; they had a "frightful, life-like gaze of exultation".

What definite meaning can we assign to such an experience and such death? On the level of folk beliefs, which we call superstition, Catherine's ghost after her death had been haunting Wuthering Heights. In her delirium, as if addressing Heathcliff, she had declared:

> I'll not lie there by myself; they may bury me twelve feet deep, and throw the church down over me, but I won't rest till you are with me. I never will!

When Heathcliff committed the wicked act of opening Catherine's coffin, her ghost caught hold of him and would not leave him. From that moment he is a man possessed and his unnatural behaviour and his death brought about by fasting and by nocturnal wanderings among the graves would be seen as the suicide of a foredoomed man. The villagers would swear that he walks and a little boy of the neighbourhood had met Heathcliff and a woman "under t' Nab". On the other hand Mrs. Dean hopes that Heathcliff sleeps soundly in his grave and the little boy "probably raised the phantoms from thinking, as he traversed the moors alone, on the nonsense he had heard his parents and companions repeat." She has not seen the ghosts; and yet, her instinct of self-preservation makes her apprehensive, so that she doesn't "like being out in the dark" or being left by herself in the grim house. The other enlightened person, Mr. Lockwood, with whose visit to the graveyard the tragic story comes to an end, wonders "how anyone could ever imagine unquiet slumbers for the sleepers in that quiet earth."

If Heathcliff and Catherine are not restless ghosts, then they are in a state of blissful union of the souls. Heathcliff's strange behaviour before his body falls is caused by the mystical exultation of a soul which is now in sight of her supreme goal. Death for such a soul is no barrier and is regarded as inconsequential; in the Shelleyan sense, it is only a veil, which, when torn, reveals the vast end everlasting ocean of love:

> Die,
> If thou wouldst be with that which thou dost seek!

After opening Catherine's coffin Heathcliff suffers from no sense of guilt; on the other hand, a strange feeling of inner contentment invests his whole being. After another visit to the grave, he tells Mrs. Dean:

> Last night, I was on the threshold of hell. Today, I am within sight of my heaven. I have my eyes on it, hardly three feet to sever me!

The great change, which Heathcliff had sensed was coming, has been seen in a different light by Arnold Kettle. He finds no mystery in it, though he says that the change is "a very subtle one". The explanation provided is not very clear. What can be gathered is that Heathcliff comes to the realisation that his methods of revenge which replicated the tactics of exploitation through money-power had proved futile :

> Only when the new change has come over Heathcliff and he again recognises through Hareton (and remotely, therefore, through Catherine herself) the full claims of humanity can Catherine be released from torment and their relationship re-established.

But the tone of the passages concerned, as well as Nelly's prophetic fear on hearing Heathcliff's revelation, does not support this interpretation: it is indeed as far-fetched as David Wilson's attempt to see Heathcliff as a representative of the rebellious working people of the hungry Forties and Catherine of those from the educated class who felt the same way.

5. The Sociological Approach

Kettle's analysis of *Wuthering Heights* is a good specimen of the sociological approach. He sees nothing mystical or romantic in the novel. The work, according to him is firmly grounded in the social reality of the time, and the people there are real people:

> *Wuthering Heights* is about England in 1847 and the years before. The people it reveals live not in a never-never land but in Yorkshire. Heathcliff was born not in the pages of Byron, but in a Liverpool slum.

He says "the centre and core of the book is the story of Catherine and Heathcliff". The torture and oppression which they suffer together as co-victims unite their beings in a union which is much deeper than romantic love. The conflict which ensues from Catherine's marrying Edgar Linton is a social conflict between two sets of values. Heathcliff and Catherine are rebels to the false bourgeois standards; that is their natural role. When Catherine allows herself to be carried away by the glamour of Thrushcross Grange norms, which are the creations of the machinery of class exploitation, she relinquishes her natural role of the rebellious victim and opts for suffering and death. Heathcliff continues to be a rebel and in possession of moral superiority; he, therefore, ought to enjoy our sympathy and admiration:

> Most of those who criticise Heathcliff adversely (on the grounds that he is unbelievable, or that he is a neurotic creation, or that he is merely the Byronic satan-hero revived) fail to appreciate his significance because they fail to recognise this moral force. And as a rule they fail to recognise the moral force, because they are themselves, consciously or not, of the Linton party.

Such polemics are often heard from the intellectuals who are themselves not qualified to advance them; they turn into self-mockery. Moreover, if the ending of the novel has any significance, Emily Brontë herself is of the Linton party, for she makes Hareton and Cathy resolve abandoning Wuthering Heights, the symbol, no doubt, of "the moral force" of Heathcliff and Catherine, and settling down at Thrushcross Grange. Kettle is certainly on the wrong track: raising Heathcliff to the status of a great revolutionary force involves tremendous contradiction and will finally amount to the advocacy of a very perverted form of Marxism which is ready to trample the basic human decencies.

As a matter of fact, Emily Brontë possesses a much deeper insight into human nature as well as social dynamics than many of her interpreters: she is prepared to look closely at the reality of Heathcliff, as a being – as *it* – and as a social entity subject to social events: and that, too, without losing her impartiality and without wincing at the sight of the terrible beauty of human passion, which verges on the inhuman and unhuman. We have already glanced at the great ambiguity connected with Heathcliff's behaviour in his last days: his state of being during that phase can be understood equally well in terms of mystical experience of bliss and in terms of 'ghost-craft', and this indeed is the final vision of human nature itself. Shakespeare-like, Emily Brontë, using the magnifying glass of her fancy, penetrates to the centre of man's being and perceives there a great mystery: man is a fascinating mixture of good and evil; the redeeming and damning elements are inextricably blended in his nature and that is the message to be gleaned from *King Lear, Othello* and many another great work of literature.

But our conventional ideas of good and evil do not operate on that level. Emily Brontë herself is conscious of a more fundamental basis of conduct than that recommended by custom. She declared in a poem (Stanzas) that she would not take the old models of action and high morality, nor would she follow the examples of the remote past whose true configurations appear distorted by the mist of the ages. She would follow her own inclination and gather her lessons from open nature – from its sources of nourishment and commotion.

Her brainchild, Catherine, also is identified with the elements of the moorland and is rooted in natural morality, it is not her marrying Edgar Linton that causes her death, but her failure to perceive the contradiction between natural and conventional morality: the kind of conflict presented by Hawthorne in *The Scarlet Letter*. Catherine's love for Heathcliff is at the level of being; she is of a piece with him; as being, Catherine, Heathcliff and the moorland are identical and inseparable. Catherine's love for Heathcliff is too strong to be manifested in romantic or erotic forms. Her love for Edgar arose out of her temporary submission to the attraction of culture and comfort and her social self's desire to provide support to Heathcliff. It is significant that she distinguishes the two kinds of love in terms of natural phenomena: the foliage that is subject to change and the eternal rocks that stand firm and immutable.

Being a true human product of amoral nature, she is distressed to see Heathcliff and Edgar ranged as bitter foes because, to her mind, the two relationships operate on two different planes and there is no question of any clash between them. She expected Heathcliff and Edgar to rise to a new height of moral standard, which they failed to do and therefore by the standards of natural morality in which

Catherine's life is grounded, the fault must be ascribed to the pettiness of the two men.

> "You and Edgar have broken my heart, Heathcliff! And you both come to bewail the deed to me, as if you were the people to be pitied! I shall not pity you, not I. You have killed me – and thriven on it, I think.

The love between Catherine and Heathcliff remains an enigma; it seems difficult to disengage it from its mystical moorings, but other rational explanations are possible. Psychoanalytically inclined critics would interpret the relationship in terms of a repressed incestuous urge and track it down to the author's attachment to her brother Branwell. Heathcliff is the brother-lover and Catherine, who represents Emily herself, must repress any explicit sign of erotic feeling towards him; the author therefore veils the emotion with a profounder but inexplicable union of the two. Once this assumption is granted the characters and events in the novel, which do not literally tally with the biographical matter can be accounted for by the dreamwork's processes of symbolisation – condensation and displacement, which operate in imaginative writing as well. One can even argue that in the love and marriage of Cathy and Hareton, there is a vicarious satisfaction of the incestuous desire.

If we do not wish to involve the author's secret life in the story, we can perhaps explain the relationship more sensibly on the psychological plane from within the novel itself. For this we'll have to turn to the childhood of Catherine and Heathcliff. Catherine is a nursling of the moors and in Heathcliff, with his ancestry of wild living, she recognises a kindred spirit. Since she was regarded as a naughty girl at home and since "Mr. Earnshaw did not understand jokes from his children", she would often run to her beloved nature in the company of Heathcliff. This seems to have been her routine for almost six years until she attained the age of twelve, when her father died. Hindley as she wrote in her journal was a detestable substitute and he let loose a reign of oppression on her and Heathcliff. Thus alienated from the family, they embarked on a course of rebellion in close association, which further strengthened their attachment. It is in this way that the natural affinity between the two young people crystallised and became firm as a rock by their communion in nature and their fellowship in suffering. For Catherine, this bond acquired a sacred character and a homogeneous aspect which made it distinct from the erotic sentiment, which is the basis of marriage. Love, for Catherine, has crossed its limits; it has gone too deep for sexuality; it has become confused with brotherly affection. In the depth of her heart she knows that Heathcliff is of a piece with her; he is not 'other'; but erotic relationship is possible only with other. Heathcliff, too, after his "enlightenment" longs to merge with Catherine into a single mass of clay. He bribed the sexton to see to it that, when he dies, his body is laid next to that of Catherine; "I'll have it made so, and then, by the time Linton gets to us, he'll not know which is which".

In spite of its spiritualistic motif, Wuthering Heights is firmly grounded in reality – the action and events of the story take place in a definite locality with pronounced geographical, topographical and demographic features. The landscape is that of the north-western moorland of England: the stunted row of firs, the gaunt thorns; Penistone crag; dogs, rabbits, moor cocks, lapwings; ghosts, fairies; the bleak hilltop and the little valley – they all belong to the real nature and humans in the vicinity of Haworth. The Elizabethan farm on the moors above Haworth is the model for Wuthering Heights. We are told that Liverpool was sixty miles away from Wuthering Heights and that Mr. Earnshaw went to the town on foot; it took him three days to complete the journey. Mr. Earnshaw could be the head of any of the agrarian families subsisting on their farms bordering the Yorkshire moors and the Lintons would be no different from the landed gentry of the region. As for Heathcliff, there is every likelihood that he was 'conceived' after hearing Branwell's accounts of the immigrant children who were starving and dying in the streets of Liverpool. The superstructure of thinking and belief is also that of a rural isolated community which retained a link with the Medieval tradition and was slowly and sporadically becoming aware of the industrial ways of man: Heathcliff most probably went away to some industrial centre where he quickly acquired money and manners; similarly Isabella, too, stayed in a town where she could provide education to her child.

The novel is equally firmly set in time: the main action covers the period from around 1771 to 1802. The time frame is foregrounded so meticulously throughout the novel that one can easily prepare a genealogical table of the principal characters: Hindley was born in 1757 and died in 1784; Catharine was born in 1765, Edgar three years earlier and Heathcliff one year earlier; Cathy was born in 1784, the year her mother died, and Hareton in the summer of 1778. We are informed that old Mr. Earnshaw undertook his journey to Livepool in a fine summer morning when Catherine was about six, that Hindley remained at college for three years, that Edgar Linton married Catharine three years after his father's death, when Hareton was nearly five years old, *i.e.* in 1783, that Catharine spent about six months in perfect peace after her marriage and then on a mellow evening in September, Heathcliff reappeared after a three-year absence – and indeed many other chronological details directly or indirectly supplied.

This novel moves on a double time-scheme: the progress of the main action in time, which as we have seen covers a period of about thirty years, and the actual telling of the story in two instalments by Mrs. Dean. Some carefully chosen parts of the story are given by Lockwood, but they are chiefly descriptive, and this links the two schemes. Lockwood took Thrushcross Grange on rent towards the close of 1801 and went to visit his landlord soon after reaching there. His second visit to Wuthering Heights involved exposure to the harsh conditions of the place which necessitated his staying indoors for a few weeks. During this period Mrs. Dean, the housekeeper related to him the tragic history of the two families from the day Old Earnshaw went to Liverpool up to the time Lockwood appeared on the scene in late 1801. In January 1802 Lockwood goes away to London for six months and in September, coming within fifteen miles of Gimmerton, he decides to visit Thrushcross Grange for one day; he is obliged to proceed to Wuthering Heights, where, in the evening he hears the remaining part of the story from Mrs. Dean – the strange end of Heathcliff and the surprising reunion of the two families in the persons of Hareton and Cathy.

When we move on to the third dimension of reality – the society – we find Emily Brontë's pen as strong in its depiction as in the delineation of place and time. The Wuthering Heights' people are farmers; they still keep an intimate bond with nature and live on its products; they lead an open-air life, supervising the farming activities and not minding to work on the field; they own cows, pigs and sheep, and go out to catch rabbits; there are horses for riding. The inside of the house described in terms of telling details clearly establishes the social status of the family as well as their life style:

> One end, indeed, reflected splendidly both light and heat from ranks of immense pewter dishes, interspersed with

> silver jugs and tankards, towering row after row, on a vast oak dresser, to the very roof. The latter had never been underdrawn: its entire anatomy lay bare to an inquiring eye, except where a frame of wood laden with oat cakes and cluster of legs of beef, mutton and ham, concealed it. Above the chimney were sundry villainous old guns, and, by way of ornament, three gaudily painted canisters disposed along its ledge. The floor was of smooth, white stone; the chairs, high-backed, primitive structures, painted green; one or two heavy black ones lurking in the shade. In an arch under the dresser, reposed a huge liver-coloured bitch pointer, surrounded by a swarm of squealing puppies; and other dogs haunted other recesses. The apartment and furniture would have been nothing extraordinary as belonging to a homely, northern farmer, with a stubborn countenance, and stalwart limbs set out to advantage in knee breeches and gaiters. Such an individual seated in his armchair, his mug of ale frothing on the round table before him, is to be seen in any circuit of five or six miles among these hills, if you go at the right time after dinner.

There would be very few domestic servants and the difference between servant and master not very great; at times it may be difficult to say whether an individual is a servant or a member of the family. When Lockwood sees Hareton at Wuthering Heights he is unable to decide his place in the household; at Thrushcross Grange there would have been no such problem. The homesteads on the countryside are situated far apart and there is little social interaction among them. But the people do share a rural cultural tradition comprising Christian ideas and moral values, folk lore and superstition. In sensibility they still maintained a continuity with Medieval England and ghosts and demons have a reality for them, though the educated minds are touched by doubt. The village folk have little to do with the expanding industrial culture, though they occasionally visit the town on special business or for buying certain kinds of articles.

On the other hand, the Linton family are landed gentry who enjoy special privileges and live in a comfortable home with a distinct sense of 'cultured' behaviour. They live elevated above the common people in better natural surroundings. We get a glimpse of Thrushcross Grange interior through Heathcliff's description. He is enthralled by the crimson-covered chairs and tables, "a pure white ceiling bordered by gold" and "glassdrops hanging in silver chains". He had seen nothing like that in Wuthering Heights. To his child's mind the room looked like heaven.

During her five weeks' stay at Thrushcross Grange, Catherine Earnshaw is transformed from a wild village girl into a lady in dress and in manners:

> I removed the habit, and there shone forth, beneath a grand plaid silk frock, white trousers and burnished shoes; and, while her eyes sparkled joyfully when the dogs came bounding up to welcome her, she dare hardly touch them lest they should fawn upon her splendid garments.

When the Linton children paid a visit to Earnshaws, they went in the family carriage "smothered in cloaks and furs". This class of people had good connections in the town; they frequently went to the city and stayed there for days together. When Isabella ran away from Wuthering Heights, she most probably sought refuge in some township near London where she remained for twelve years; her son Linton was born and brought up in the urban milieu and he had the habits of a town child.

There are many other pictures of reality such as only a great painter in words like Chaucer could manage. The homes of the people are described in such a manner that they clearly reflect the economic and social distinctions and the characters themselves are at once individual and representative. But the Marxist critics won't stop at that; below this surface reality, they perceive the forces of class interests engaged in constant struggle and torn by contradictions – and making for social transformation.

Arnold Kettle, as we have seen, seeks to demystify the theme; according to him it symbolically represents the clash between the solid socio-economic interests of the suppressed class represented by Heathcliff and those of the bourgeoisie.

> The story of Wuthering Heights is concerned not with love in the abstract but with the passions of living people, with property ownership, the attraction of social comforts, the arrangement of marriages, the importance of education, the validity of religion, the relations of rich and poor.

Heathcliff is a conscious rebel against the shallow bourgeois values and conventions as regards love and social respectability; that is why he retains our sympathy in spite of his atrocious dealings and Emily Brontë meant it so. Catherine in this matter is his natural ally and her desertion of him in favour of the comfortable and elegant life at the Grange was a false step which led to her tragedy. Heathcliff himself sought to pay his oppressors in their own coin, but after capturing the properties of the two families, when he finds a new order taking shape in the relationship between Cathy and Hareton, he realises that in social terms he had been fighting a losing battle; he becomes thoroughly disillusioned and loses the will to live.

Terry Eagleton in his Marxist study of the Brontës is more penetrating in his analysis. He seeks to uncover the ideological basis of their work and to relate their productions to their situation in the society. He borrows the concept of 'categorial structure' from the Marxist critic Lucien Goldman, "who uses it to designate those shared categories which inform apparently heterogeneous works, and shape the consciousness of the particular social group or class which produces them". As understood by Eagleton, this involves finding out the inner ideological structure of a work and exposing its relations to both literary form and to an actual history. "That ideological structure" he says, "arises from the real history of the West Riding in the first half of the nineteenth century; and it is, I believe, imaginatively grasped and transposed in the production of the Brontës' fiction". Historically the major conflict is that between landed and industrial capital, but it is "sharpened and complicated for the Brontës by a host of subsidiary factors".

The Brontë sisters, each according to her genius and perception, embodied in literary form the predicament of their social situation and the rebellious feelings of their class. They lived isolated lives in a remote northern parsonage and socially as well as economically they were insecure women. Economically, they had to serve others as governesses in order to keep themselves alive, but educationally they were superior to the very families to whom they were little more than servants. Their lives were based in the agrarian world whose values and satisfactions were under attack by industrialism. In the Brontës, Eagleton finds "an abnormally stark opposition between a kind of 'pre-industrial' imaginative creativity, feeding off the resources of myth, archetype, rhetoric, melodrama and the felt pressures of a drably spiritless society to which that imagination must either tortuously adapt or suffer extinction."

In *Wuthering Heights*, Eagleton reorganises several of the contradictions of the contemporary society as felt and imaginatively transcribed by Emily Brontë. The primary contradiction for him (as well as for Kettle, as noted earlier) is "the choice posed for Catherine between Heathcliff and Edgar Linton". Heathcliff, it may be noted, represents, at this point in the story, the agrarian working class and Edgar the landed gentry. Heathcliff later acquires economic power and is assimilated to the capitalist forces. His career spells out the ambivalent relationship existing at the time between the industrial bourgeoisie and the landed gentry. "His rise to power symbolises at once the triumph of the oppressed over capitalism and the triumph of capitalism over the oppressed." Heathcliff is at once progressive and outdated: he is opposed to the capitalist forces of Thrushcross Grange, but he uses their methods to the limit of parody. "He behaves in this way because his 'soul' belongs not to that world but to Catherine; and in that sense his true commitment is an 'outdated' one, to a past increasingly mythical realm of absolute personal value which capitalist social relations cancel".

Eagleton also perceives in the novel a contradiction between nature and society. Nature is simultaneously inside and outside society: "at one level it represents the unsalvaged region beyond the pale of culture; at another level it signifies the all pervasive reality of which culture itself is a particular outcropping".

Ralph Fox regards the novel, as a genre, to be the supreme artistic achievement of the capitalist order; in the work of Rebelais and Cervantes, Feilding and Smollett, it became the epic of the people, able to depict man in reality and in all aspects. Paradoxically, after gaining power in the eighteenth century, that very order destroyed the conditions in which realism could prosper. It imposed restrictions on a full and true portrayal of man; human nature could be treated in art, specially the novel, only in its distorted and truncated form. In the nineteenth century, the centralisation of capital gave rise to new human relations which were both false and shallow; as a consequence, the sensitive mind of the creative writer felt distressed, rebellious and alienated. Most writers surrendered themselves to the oppressive system and many talented ones were obliged to compromise their art to the bourgeois values. But a few courageous novelists bitterly challenged the dehumanised image of man and presented human relations in a different light – Emily Brontë was one of them. *Wuthering Heights* is a great novel according to Fox because it is the cry of pain that life itself wrenched from Emily's heart. The mid-Victorian England gave birth to this novel. It was essential for Emily that love must achieve a total victory, and so it did in the atmosphere of violence and fear in the stone-house on the moors. The characters of Catherine and Heathcliff symbolise love's revenge on the nineteenth century.

These brief general comments are perhaps more helpful in understanding the nature and spirit of the social conflict than the detailed analyses written by Kettle and Eagleton. Those analyses seem to involve some distortion in the intention of the author as revealed by the tone and also in the actual social reality: 'Capitalism, 'bourgeoise', and 'oppressed class' are big words to use in the context of isolated families in the moorland and Emily Brontë herself did not perceive the situation in precise Marxist terms so as to project Heathcliff as a class-hero.

The author and her hero, Heathcliff – both attained important Marxist insights, namely, that the prevailing values of the society are imposed and shallow, that they are tools of oppression in the hands of the masters of property, that the true and natural feelings and attachments between men and women are stigmatised in this order and that one ought to rise in rebellion against the established system. But at the same time, it is evident that Heathcliff has no clear perception of the issues in Marxist terms; nor has Emily, because both of them, for good or for ill, stray into the realm of the spiritual and make it the basis of their life's course and purpose. Heathcliff pursues a double aim: to reunite his soul with Catherine's and to take revenge on the two families by adopting those very means – private ownwership and legal trickery – which he is supposed to attack and replace.

6. The Middle Path

We have spent a great deal of time with the learned discussions of *Wuthering Heights*. Let us now see whether we can contribute something to the understanding and evaluation of the novel in our capacity as experienced readers who have learnt by practice how to enjoy and appreciate a literary work. What are the things in the novel that appeal to us and what prompts us to conclude that it is a great work of literature?

The first thing to be noticed is that *Wuthering Heights* has one of the most powerful openings; there are very few other works of literature which take hold of our mind so completely. In the first two chapters the reader is plunged into a situation which, on every hand, bristles with mystery; and with Lockword, an outsider like ourselves, we are puzzled and make errors of judgement. Heathcliff, to all appearances, is a specimen of educated humanity, and yet in his dealings he far outpaces Lockwood in his aversion to society; and in rudeness, he has no equal. Naturally, Lockwood "felt interested in a man who seemed more exaggeratedly reserved than myself". Heathcliff remains till the end the prime object of our deep curiosity and the mystery of his being is not solved even after we have closed the book.

Hardly have we recovered from the first shock when another enigma is wheeled into focus in the form of a young lady, "scarcely past girlhood", who is the mistress of very charming features. But the only sentiment her attractive eyes gave vent to "hovered between scorn and a kind of desperation, singularly unnatural to be detected there." She behaves mechanically like a pre-programmed automaton. Later, Lockwood makes several mistakes in guessing her identity. Lockwood's romantic interest in this figure is a source of curiosity to the reader until Hareton unexpectedly steps in as a lover. Hareton himself is no less opaque: in his talk and dress he appears to be an uneducated labourer; his figure also suggests a weather-beaten farm-hand; but in his bearing he displays pride and independence with no touch of servility towards the lady of the house.

There are two other powerful factors which greatly intensify our feeling of curiosity. The details of the surroundings presented to us are rather peculiar:

> Pure, bracing ventilation they must have up there at all times, indeed; one may guess the power of the north wind blowing over the edge, by the excessive slant of a few stunted firs at the end of the house, and by a range of gaunt thorns all stretching their limbs one way, as if craving alms of the sun.

The force of nature operates here in its full strength imparting an eccentric momentum to everything that it touches and this, we are told, is the dwelling of Mr. Heathcliff. The description widens the scope of our curiosity and also makes an appeal to the deepest level of the mind by introducing certain elements – urges and oppositions – which constitute the very being of man and which connect human nature with cosmic nature. The common reader, most probably, does not consciously analyse the symbolism and imagery of the passage in order to take in the effect: the perception is intuitive and the appeal directly strikes the unconscious mind, whose autochthonous tendency finds satisfaction in it. This means that the watertight division between man and nature is being demolished.

Chapter 3 adds the second factor, which undermines the boundary between life and death. Lockwood's nightmarish confrontation with Catherine is delicately poised between dream and reality; the description of the experience is one of the greatest achievements of literary craftsmanship. Here, if anywhere, ambiguity is put to the best use:

> I listened doubtingly an instant; detected the disturber, then turned and dosed, and dreamt again: if possible, still more disagreeably than before.
>
> This time, I remembered I was lying in the oak closet, and I heard distinctly the gusty wind and the driving of the snow; I heard also, the fir bough repeat its teasing sound, and ascribed it to the right cause; but it annoyed me so much, that I resolved to silence it, if possible; and, I thought, I rose and endeavoured to unhasp the casement. The hook was soldered into the staple, a circumstance observed by me when awake, but forgotten. "I must stop it, nevertheless"! I muttered, knocking my knuckles through the glass, and stretching an arm out to seize the importunate branch; instead of which, my fingers closed on the fingers of a little ice-cold hand!

The curiosity value of the 'dream' is beyond any doubt. Lockwood himself is convinced that the house is haunted: "I'm not going to endure the persecutions of your hospitable ancestors again", he told Heathcliff later. He is full of revulsion at the time, but the people of Wuthering Heights have taken such a hold of his mind that he is prepared to forego rest and food in order to hear their strange tale. In the first three chapters, the clock of the tale is wound so tightly that it will take a long time for its spring to relax, but in the meantime, as already indicated, a much deeper involvement has arisern and it will take us forward beyond the point where our curiosity is mollified.

Wuthering Heights is not escape fiction and it does not dole out programmed sensationalism merely to send shivers down our spine.

We do not find in it secret passages and magic doors; and the dead unbelievably stretching their leperous hands towards us and beaming at us their ghastly smiles. Things in this novel are managed within the broad framework of reality and the unusual happenings are dubiously placed in the shadowy border between this world and the other: there is no shattering shock to the rational faculty of the mind; and yet the shadow of the other world is never absent. Reason is never allowed to find itself completely in command of the 'reality' it is confronted with. It is marked off unambiguously from a thriller by its serious concern with the motive elements that operate in the cosmos, human heart and the society with their fierce collision and evolutionary harmony achieved after violence and suffering. In short, it attempts to interpret some fundamental issues of life, which lie beneath the surface reality and unite the whole human race in time and space by means of shared inherited traits common to all.

First of these issues is the nature of human passion in its awful amoral magnitude and its conflict with the norms of the polite society. It is the manifestation in man of nature's vital force which is fully contented as long as the lovers enjoy each other's company in the ambience of nature; so long as the lovers remain united, the woes inflicted by the world are of no account. This adamantine bond between two souls is no beggar at the door of kisses and caresses; it is not dependent on sexual traction, the two souls can never be separated: "Nelly, I am Heathcliff!" cries Catherine, and forbids her to talk of separation for "it is impracticable". And for Heathcliff, Catherine is never absent. The physical separation of the lovers is like the dividing of a mountain river which then turns violent chafing and fuming against the hurdles until the two streams are rejoined.

This elemental force of cohesion is contrasted with the sentiment called love in the conventional parlance. Love in the genteel society is a weak emotion with neither depth nor strength and in the final analysis is smeared with selfishness. Heathcliff exposes with bitter sarcasm the hollowness of Edgar's love for Catherine:

> And that insipid, paltry creature attending her from duty and humanity! He might as well plant an oak in a flower-pot, and expect it to thrive, as imagine he can restore her to vigour in the soil of his shallow cares!

Heathcliff's scorn for Edgar's love has been theorised by some scholars into Emily Brontë's contempt for the values of the bourgeois society, but that conclusion will not only misrepresent the author but also misinterpret the novel. Perhaps, the common reader, unbiased by theorising, is in a better position to judge the character of Edgar and what he stands for in the true perspective – and then there are his own knowledge and experience to assist him in estimating. In human terms Heathcliff's character is at a disadvantage when compared with Edgar's capacity for tolerance, his concern for Catherine except when he is kept in dark by Mrs. Dean, and his devotion to his daughter, Cathy. These are the qualities which cannot be dismissed as "shallow cares"; they are distinctive human values.

In fact, Emily Brontë is wiser than her interpreters and she is again dealing with the contradictory pulls of two most radical urges of the human mind: hence her widest appeal to the reader. She is concerned with two basic urges which may be termed 'nature' and 'culture'; with man's tendency to follow nature, to be an extension of nature, to return to nature and his tendency to be independent of nature, to build his own system of behaviour and value. Human life pulsates between these two poles, is subject to their force, and occasionally, through the evolutionary process, finds a synthesis of the two which is the source of joyful life, such as Hareton and Cathy begin to lead towards the end of the novel.

The theorist may ignore the power of the second urge, culture, as represented in the novel, or call it superficial bourgeois construct, but the common reader who is steeped in social intercourse and aspiration will not dismiss it as of no account. Heathcliff himself is attracted by its elegance. We have seen how the drawing room of the Lintons impressed him – its warmth, its comfort, its colours. He also found Edgar's personality superior to his own:

> But, Nelly, If I knocked him down twenty times, that wouldn't make him less handsome or me more so. I wish I had light hair and a fair skin and was dressed and behaved as well, and had a chance of being as rich as he will be!

And when Heathcliff disappeared from Wuthering Heights, he must have gone in search of some of the things that Edgar possessed; he could not acquire light hair and a fair skin, but he did return well-dressed, well-behaved when he chose, and rich.

As regards Catherine's response, she, too, came under the sway of culture during her short stay at the Grange – both its superficial and the human aspects. She noticeably became conscious of her dress and status: while shaking hands with Heathcliff "she gazed concernedly at the dusky fingers she held in her own, and also at her dress, which she feared had gained no embellishment from its contact with his". Traversi has observed: "The part of Catherine's nature which craves civilized, social fulfilment is sufficiently attracted by the agreeable aspects of life in the society of the Lintons to marry Edgar and become part of the family. She never refuses the name of 'love' for her feeling for Edgar." After her marriage, Catherine continued to be true to herself because nature is not inclined to be compromising, but culture possesses the virtue of flexibility: "It was not the thorn bending to the honeysuckle, but the honeysuckle embracing the thorn." Thus although the effort to accommodate was onesided, the outcome happened to be entirely wholesome. Nelly Dean who watched the young couple every hour is prepared to assert "that they were really in possession of deep and growing happiness".

Yet culture does fail the final acid test. Catherine who perceived her relationships to Heathcliff and Edgar on two separate planes had expected the latter to make his peace with the former for her sake: "Edgar must shake off his antipathy, and tolerate him, at least. He will, when he learns my true feelings towards him." But this perhaps is too much to ask. The demand made would require a much higher standard of culture: that, as every common man knows, would need a saint. Neither can nature make such adjustment; in fact it is incapable of doing so. Heathcliff as a child had felt great contempt for Edgar and Isabella when he found them quarrelling over a little dog and he rhetorically asked Nelly: "When would you catch me wishing to have what Catherine wanted?" But does he actually live up to that assertion? Nature, perhaps, by its very nature is incapable of accepting a rival in love and sex.

It will have become clear by now that nature *versus* culture is a great theme in the novel and it makes a universal appeal. Traversi, from whose article we have already quoted, has dealt with this contrast in roughly the same terms and he thinks it "lies at the heart of the novel". David Cecil's theory of the conflicting principles of Storm and Calm is also not totally unrelated to the contrast discussed above.

The ending of the novel is particularly interesting; it is also controversial. But before we discuss its appeal, we must note that it is in fact a double ending. First, it presents a happy outcome of the bitter antagonism between the two houses of Wuthering Heights and Thrushcross Grange representing two kinds of temperament with their respective strong points and defects. The evolutionary process and suffering have "treated" each strain in such a manner that its tragic projections, which were sure to stand in the way of mutual bliss, at least in this world as we know it, have got smoothened through intermixture. In the last scene of this saga of three generations on either side, we find the scions of the two families coming together and falling in love with each other in spite of, or perhaps partly because of, Heathcliff's endeavours to the contrary – perhaps it will not be wholly fantastic to suggest that, like an inverted Prospero, Heathcliff had unconsciously wished for this kind of fulfilment.

There can be no doubt that the common reader rejoices in the union of the two families in the persons of Hareton and Cathy. The specialist may grumble and say that the ending is contrived and that the author has compromised her art to public taste. This criticism, however, is unfair. It requires no more than a careful reading to see that what passes between Hareton and Cathy before they 'know' each other is the result of childish prejudice and misunderstanding and not of ingrained hatred – the latter feeling alone could preclude the possibility of a happy relationship: "I don't mean anything, I don't mean that I despise you. Come, you shall take notice of me, Hareton – you are my cousin, and you shall own me." We must not forget that Hareton and Cathy hit if off very well with each other in a romantic landscape. At Penistone Crags Hareton was Cathy's guide and he "opened the mysteries of the Fairy cave, and twenty other queer places", though the young lady being cross with Nelly, refused to disclose all the details to her. Until the social factor pushed them apart, Hareton had been a favourite of Cathy and as two human creatures they began by liking each other. And at the time of parting, Hareton made an attempt at *rapprochement* by putting a fine crooked-legged terrier whelp into her hand. Later on when Cathy was forced to live in Wuthering Heights, Heathcliff's attitude towards her and her own haughtiness helped to keep the two souls apart. Gradually, however, Hareton, in his own way, began to give signs of his inner feeling of love for her; trying to be presentable, picking books for her from the sideboard, stroking her hair, surrendering Nelly Dean's letter that he had seized. Hareton was ready to become a patient bookworm for Cathy's sake as Prince Ferdinand had become a patient logman for Miranda's sake. But the greatest heroic deed on his part was to defend Cathy from the assault of Heathcliff, his spiritual father. As regards Cathy's teasing of Hareton, that is an amorous device as old as Eve – Didn't she tease Adam into committing the act which made love in this world practicable? Moreover, when we consider the wretched situation in which the two were placed – a virtual confinment – at a place which otherwise also offered no society, it becomes not only highly probable but also inevitable that they should eventually move closer to each other.

From the point of view of our imaginative experience, since this ending is far from an ethereal flight of the fancy, it comes as a soothing balm to the heart and since the imaginative experience must answer for the artistic form, artistically too, it is flawless. Love has ultimately emerged victorious; it has triumphed over violence and hatred: Heathcliff has surrendered under its two-pronged force and is preparing himself for death in order to achieve union with Catherine in body and soul. This positive note whose music fills the last chapters of the book is a vital element and it is a great support the human spirit is always in need of.

The other part of the ending pertains to the superhuman passion of Heathcliff and Catherine. This passion, surging forth like a giant wave, does not respect the constraint of death. Emily Brontë has been raising the viewing stand of our mind to that requisite cosmic height from which the last scene can be seen in its awful grandeur; Catherine with admirable intuition spoke to Mrs. Dean about the universal wish for a life beyond this world: "I cannot express it; but surely you and everybody have a notion that there is or should be an existence of yours beyond you. What were the use of my creation if I were entirely contained here?" In her delirium, she addresses Heathcliff saying: "I'll not lie there by myself; they may bury me twelve feet deep, and throw the church down over me, but I won't rest till you are with me. I never will!" Heathcliff is also entrenched in the same belief. As his end approaches his heart fills with a strange excitement; he is eager to meet death because that is no final curtain; it must lift to facilitate his progress further in the direction of his love.

The end of the love story of Heathcliff and Catherine – more appropriately, its consummation – comes just as it should. We know from our experience of the world that the thwarted love of such a superhuman proportion cannot have a happy ending in the normal sense of the phrase, but when the barrier of death is removed by the power of the creative imagination as it is in *Wuthering Heights*, the spirits comingle happily and are in peace that passes understanding.

Emily Brontë's treatment of the life beyond death is a source of fascination, for she deals with the theme in the spirit of medieval balladry. Many of these ballads having a primitive element in them exercise a peculiar charm on the reader and they are popular in spite of – perhaps because of – their unbelievable supernatural machinery. This is because we probably still retain somewhere in our psyche that ancient self to which ghosts, goblins and fiends, as well as gods and angels, were part of the reality – the self that was aware of the fourth dimension of life. Or we perhaps still relish to see our wishes and fears embodied in surreal forms through our imagination.

In *Wuthering Heights* we don't meet lovers long past dead, magicians turning themselves into birds and beasts, the drowned sons of a woman visiting her in the middle of the night and melting into air at cockcrow, but Emily Brontë constantly lets the other shadowy world knock at the door with its sinister gestures. Mr. Lockwood an educated man of the age of science is so confused by his terrifying experience at Wuthering Heights that he declares the house is haunted. In us too, the power of evocation applied by Emily revives an ancient mind – a mind which believed in ghosts and demons. And perhaps that antique mind has not yet died out completely in us. The surrounding nature with its Penistone Cargs and Fairy Caves pulsates with a strange being, and Heathcliff and Catherine frequently plant their other foot in the other world. Nelly Dean, recounting the cowboy's frightening experience, nervously comments:

> He probably raised the phantoms from thinking, as he traversed the moors alone, on the nonsense he had heard his parents and companions repeat – yet still, I don't like being out in the dark, now; and I don't like being left by myself in this grim house – I cannot help it.....

Nor can we, once we walk into the charmed circle of Emily Brontë. The local characters through whose consciousness we enter the experience of the novel are touched by the shadowy plane of being, and chief of them is Nelly Dean. The language and imagery habitually used by these persons keep signing towards things outside the ordinary and the normal and we find in them a strange marriage of Heaven and Hell. Offering the swarthy infant to his wife old Earnshaw says, "You must e'en take it as a gift of God, though it's as dark almost as if it came from the devil." Irate Hindley, surrendering his colt to Heathcliff, exclaims: "take him, and be damned, you beggarly interloper! and wheedle my father out of all he has; only afterwards show him what you are, imp of Satan!" Quarrelling with Edgar, Isabella was shrieking "as if witches were running red-hot needles into her". Seeing that the bulldog of Lintons had seized Catherine's ankles, Heathcliff "vociferated curses enough to annihilate any fiend in Christendom". Nelly Dean admonishes Catherine saying that they were "dismal enough without conjuring up ghosts and visions". Catherine dreamt that she was in heaven, but it did not seem to be her home, she began weeping and the angels were so angry that they threw her out. Isabella wonders whether Heathcliff is a man; "If so, is he mad? And if not, is he a devil"; she wants to know "what" she has married. Hindley contemplates recovering his lost property from Heathcliff: "I'll have his gold too : and then his blood; and hell shall have his soul".

Finally, in his last phase of excitement, Heathcliff becomes a great mystery: it is impossible to say whether he is in possession of the heavenly bliss or is himself possessed by an evil spirit: "Heathcliff stood at the open door; he was pale, and he trembled, yet, certainly, he had a strange joyful glitter in his eyes that altered the aspect of his whole face". A few hours later Nelly Dean noticed "the same unnatural – it was unnatural – appearance of joy under his black brows". When questioned about his strange condition Heathcliff reveals: "Last night, I was on the threshold of hell. Today, I'm within sight of my heaven". This does not clear the matter, for how are we to interpret, "my heaven". A little later, after watching Heathcliff's face, Nelly is again assailed by fearful doubt and uncertainty:

> "Is he a ghost, or a vampire?" I mused. I had read of such hideous, incarnate demons. And then I set myself to reflect how I had tended him in infancy; and watched him grow to youth, and followed him almost through his whole course; and what absurd nonsense it was to yield to that sense of terror.
>
> 'But where did he come from, the little dark thing, harboured by a good man to his bane?' muttered superstition, as I dozed into unconsciousness.

Even after his death, Heathcliff's corpse presented a vision of good and evil hopelessly confused and the reader can only marvel at the converging ways of heaven and hell. The element of demonology, if you like, extending from beginning to end, lends a powerful attraction to the novel, but it is not definitive; unlike terror novel, *Wuthering Heights*, goes much deeper and explores the mysteries of love, life and death; it also challenges our conventional ideas of good and evil.

The other aspect of the novel which must appeal to the reader is its convincing development. Given in bare outline, the plot is incredible, studied in detail its unravelling is almost inevitable: every outcome has a reasonable explanation.

We begin with the thesis that nature's forces have the power to determine human temperament; they impart their own qualities to their human proteges. The two extreme milieux are the high places and the valley of the northern moorland. In accordance with this theorem, Wuthering Heights has fathered and formed the Earnshaws who possess a strongly passionate and eccentric temperament; and they are unpredictable. It is, therefore, not surprising that old Earnshaw should pick up a waif from the streets of Liverpool and bring him home. But there is also a hidden motive; being not very happy with Hindley, old Earnshaw must have felt keenly the loss of another son who died in childhood and his suppressed wish must have suddenly prompted him to pick up the orphan and call him Heathcliff, the name given to the son who had died. Heathcliff himself, although an outsider, is a Wuthering Heights temperament: gipsy features, wildness, strong will.

Seeing the uncouth, sudden stranger and knowing that they have lost their gifts on account of him, Hindley and Catherine react strongly against him, and when the master begins to show undue partiality to the boy, Hindley, being a male and heir, develops a permanent antipathy towards the intruder. Knowing what children are, we must agree that this reaction is quite natural. Hindley's feeling of hatred is further strengthened by Catherine's growing intimacy with Heathcliff. Catherine, being of the opposite sex, soon got rid of her childish dislike for Heathcliff and was powerfully drawn to him, because, he too was a nursling of wild nature; and after being rejected by Hindley, Mrs. Earnshaw and the servants he preferred to stay out of doors in the company of Catherine.

This initial imbroglio will take us some way into the story and provide convincing justification for many future events. But further complications are certainly required. We shall not go into all the details because a close reading of the text itself will reveal the causes and effects. We must, however, glance at some important developments. The entry of the Linton children into the story creates a major complication which has a symmetrical pattern, for they represent the other pole in human society – what we have broadly called culture. Just at the time when Heathcliff stands utterly humiliated and brutalised and deliberately tries to be nasty, his opposite force – this pole of culture – strikes with its full impact: it is no wonder that Catherine should weaken and be drawn towards the glamour of high living. At a later point Isabella's infatuation with Heathcliff can be explained in terms of the same pull in the opposite direction – towards the strong and violent. Catherine's union with Edgar produces its fruit of welcome synthesis in the person of their daughter and this in turn flowers into benign love between Cathy and Hareton.

The other major consequence, namely, the death of Heathcliff, could almost be foretold: separated from nature and Heathcliff, Catherine could not breath and when Catherine is dead, Heathcliff's death would be a foregone conclusion. Thus viewed, the plot of *Wuthering Heights* turns out to be a concatenation of perfectly sensible causes and effects. Even the supernatural factor is so well controlled that it can be explained on rational grounds in terms of the prevailing atmosphere, tension and extreme dispositions.

We must not, however, assume that the supernatural intimations are merely marginal; not at all, the novel does not give us time to think of any rational explanation: its supreme achievement is to make us conscious of the other reality and the rational alternative is kept open in order to prevent us from regarding the novel as just another terror story written to provide the luxury of a negative sensation – far from this, *Wuthering Heights* forcefully asserts the reality of a spiritual sphere of being.

7. Narrative Technique and Mode of Perception

A. Mastery of Form

Commenting on Emily Brontë's mastery of form, David Cecil has remarked that "she had not only an imagination of the first order, she was also a consummate artist." First, she possessed artistic integrity which means "the power to keep within her imaginative range", and secondly she had the sense of form. He defines her method as "dramatic-pictorial" and shows how her presentation serves its purpose. According to Walter Allen, she not only anticipates Conrad's method of narration, she even goes further:

> *Wuthering Heights* is anything but botched: The conception is matched by a technique equally superb. To find anything to rival it we have to wait for the arrival of Conrad half a century later; in fact, Emily Brontë anticipates uncannily Conrad's characteristic methods of narrative as we find them in *Lord Jim* and *Chance* and goes into even subtler degrees of complexity.
>
> (*The English Novel*)

B. Narrators

Let us therefore engage in working out the implications of these judgements by actually looking into the narrative structure of the novel and ascertaining the purpose and effect of each move. We are often told that the task of narration is shared by Lockwood and Nelly Dean, both of whom are detached observers. It will therefore be something of a shock to be told that as far as the story is concerned there is no author in it and no one narrates it to the reader and that neither Lockwood nor Nelly Dean is a wholly detached observer.

Lockwood is an urban man confined within the bounds of skin-deep emotions, superficial interests and undaring involvement. He is a Prufrockian character *sans* Prufrock's intellectual depth and learning. But in spite of these handicaps he does become involved in the situation both intellectually and emotionally. First he is stung into a burning curiosity by stumbling against a character who is miles ahead of him in what he conceived of as misanthropy. He is also suddenly wheeled into a world of harsh and forbidding nature, fierce emotions, inherited syndromes and adamantine bonds. Secondly his heart is attracted by the young widow whom he characteristically perceives in terms of romance. His unexpressed thought reveals his involvement better than the questions he put to Nelly Dean:

> 'Oh, I'll turn the talk on my landlord's family!' I thought to myself. 'A good subject to start and that pretty girl-widow, I should like to know her history, whether she be a native of the country, or, as is more probable, an exotic that the surely indigenae will not recognise for kin.

Earlier, Lockwood had observed Cathy's face and figure somewhat closely and described for himself her beautiful features – something remarkable in a novel where detailed descriptions of characters (even major characters) are not to be found.

> She was slender, and apparently scarcely past girlhood: an admirable form, and the most exquisite little face that I have ever had the pleasure of beholding: small features, very fair; flaxen ringlets, or rather golden, hanging loose on her delicate neck; and eyes, had they been agreeable in expression, they would have been irresistible.

On his second visit itself, Lockwood began thinking of Cathy in relation to himself. His feelings towards her, however shallow, are unmistakable from his reaction to the guess that she is married to Hareton: "Here is the consequence of being buried alive: she has thrown herself away upon that boor, from sheer ignorance that better individuals existed!" – meaning himself.

As the saying goes, love and hatred cannot be concealed. To the experienced eye of Nelly Dean, the signs were quite clear. Lockwood had a picture of Cathy installed over his fireplace and whenever her name was mentioned he looked so lively and interested. When confronted with these questions, he is impelled to give went to his true feelings:

> 'Stop, my good friend!' I cried. It may be very possible that I should love her; but would she love me? I doubt it too much to venture my tranquility by running into temptation: and them my home is not here.

This is very characteristic of Lockwood's personality: like Prufrock he is torn by hesitation and apprehension:

> Would it have been worthwhile
> If one, settling a pillow or throwing off a shawl,
> And turning toward the window, should say:
> 'That is not it at all,
> That is not what I meant, at all.'
>
> (The Love Song of Alfred J. Prufrock)

Lockwood is given aware that his inclination towards Cathy may not have gone unnoticed. That is why, while handing over a letter from Mrs. Dean, he prefaced his act by saying, "A letter from your old acquaintance, the housekeeper at the Grange", fearful lest it should be taken for a letter from himself. His last wish before leaving for London was to get a glimpse of Cathy, which could not be satisfied; still, he wistfully cogitated, "what a realisation of something more romantic than a fairy tale it would have been for Mrs. Heathcliff, had she and I struck up an attachment, as her good nurse desired, and migrated together into the stirring atmosphere of the town". On his last brief visit to Wuthering Heights, Lockwood faced a revelation, described as zestfully by the author – Cathy and Hareton amiably occupied and he knew that he had once again lost the game through inaction: "and I bit my lip, in spite, at having thrown away the chance I might have had of doing something besides staring at its smiting beauty".

Nelly Dean is no more detached than Lockwood. Critics have noted her involvement in the story – even to the extent of influencing the course of events and contributing to the tragedy. She had grown up with the children of old Earnshaw and when the old Master promised gifts to his children she was not excluded; her deep attachment extended to the other house after Catherine's marriage to Edgar Linton. Her deep love for Hareton and younger Catherine is most eloquently expressed in her own words. When Hindley died she wept as for a brother:

> I confess this blow was greater to me than the shock of Mrs. Linton's death: ancient associations lingered round my heart; I sat down in the porch and wept as for a blood relation, desiring Kenneth to get another servant to introduce him to the master.

Her lapses in action and attitude are not inconsiderable. She did not take the growing conflict between Hindley and Heathcliff seriously and did nothing to assuage it. Had she cautioned Catherine about the presence of Heathcliff as soon as she detected it, while the former was telling her that it would degrade her to marry Heathcliff, things may not have gone beyond repair; instead she told a lie and when she did reveal the truth, it was too late. When Catherine was really sick and very sore that Edgar did not bother about her, Nelly Dean misinformed both the parties. These are some of the instances which prove that Mrs. Dean is more than an impartial detached narrator.

The purpose of the foregoing discussion was to stress a point which has an important bearing on the craft of fiction. It shows that Emily Brontë possessed a deeper insight into the mechanics of fiction than many a modern novelist. She knew that a totally uncommitted and detached narrator is psychologically unconvincing and would affect the quality and level of the narrative. Motivated and emotionally involved narrators, in spite of their limited view of reality are more natural and plausible. They save the art from becoming mere artifice. An impartial narrator who noticed the events out of mere intellectual curiosity or generosity would be little more than a narrating machine; it is also hard to believe that he can sustain himself through a long telling with unflagging interest and enthusiasm.

C. As Revelation

But we have ventured the statement that in *Wuthering Heights* there is no narrator in the technical sense. In explaining this assertion we shall first turn to a certain proposition in modern fiction criticism in the hope of discovering how to 'feel' this novel as a whole. A genuine novel, it is argued, teaches the reader how to approach it and it provides a key to its fictional technique and how it is to be experienced. Analysing *Tristam Shandy* in a well-known article, Victor Shklovsky says that it is characteristic of Sterne to lay bare his technique. He holds that *Tristam Shandy* is distinguished by its capacity to draw attention to the required fictional devices and modes of perception. Referring to *Ulysses* in his book *Structuralism in Literature* Robert Scholes has stressed that "in reading it we learn how to read it."

Now this exactly is the issue that ought to be explored in relation to *Wuthering Heights*: it is a novel that teaches us how to read it – how to react to its theme and technique, which coalesce under our very eyes as our reading proceeds. To learn this lesson in method and perception, we must turn to the ghostly situation in Chapter 3. The atmosphere is best presented in Emily Brontë's own words, and the passage is so crucial that it has to be quoted in full and studied closely:

> The ledge, where I placed my candle, had a few mildewed books piled up in one corner, and it was covered with writing scratched on the paint. This writing, however, was nothing but a name repeated in all kinds of characters, large and small – *Catherine Earnshaw*, here and there varied to *Catherine Heathcliff*, and then again to *Catherine Linton*.
>
> In vapid listlessness I leant my head against the window,

> and continued spelling over Catherine Earnshaw-Heathcliff-Linton, till my eyes closed; but they had not rested five minutes when a glare of white letters started from the dark, as vivid as spectres – the air swarmed with Catherines; and rousing myself to dispel the obtrusive name, I discovered my candle wick reclining on one of the antique volumes, and perfuming the place with an odour of roasted calfskin. I snuffed it off, and very ill at ease under the influence of cold and lingering nausea, sat up and spread open the injured tome on my knee. It was a Testament, in lean type, and smelling dreadfully musty: a fly-leaf bore, the inscription – Catherine Earnshaw, her book and a date some quarter of a century back.

The passage is highly symbolic: it recreates a closed corner of hell with tunnell-like coach, decaying things, musty air, foul smell of smouldering calfskin, and enveloping darkness. But what is most important – and ought not to be overlooked – in the midst of this eerie setting is the manner in which the quintessence of the novel appears to Lockwood, and to the reader, for the latter, at this stage, has no other character to identify with except Lockwood; and Lockwood, being an ordinary educated man from the city is very much like the average reader of fiction.

Catherine Earnshaw, Catherine Heathcliff, Catherine Linton – the life of Catherine, inside and outside, beginning to end, strikes the consciousness of Lockwood with the force of a mystical vision – a revelatory cryptogram. It is like a code requiring interpretation and it appears in an unusual form: scratched on the paint – a writing on the wall. Lest he miss the significance of the sign, the vision strikes him again in the form of a lurid visual image – "a glare of white letters started from the dark, as vivid as spectres". Thus is revealed "Catherine Earnshaw, her book", and Lockwood is impelled to read Catherine's journal.

This imitation of Lockwood into the technique and the meaning of an extraordinary experience, is paradigmatic and can serve as a lesson to be learnt by the reader in approaching the experience encoded in *Wuthering Heights*:

> 1801 – I have just returned from a visit to my landlord – the solitary neighbour that I shall be troubled with. This is certainly a beautiful country!

The pages of somebody's journal begin to open suddenly in front of our eyes very much like the journal of Catherine Earnshaw. The purpose is not to inform any outsider – the reader is not addressed – but to record an extraordinary experience. No one has come forward to establish a channel of communication, because strictly speaking there is no narrator: Lockwood is writing for himself because he has been stirred to the depth of his being by a new kind of reality. We are called upon to 'feel' the story as a vision; and if we have not taken it that way, Lockwood's own encounter with Catherine's story forces us to correct our stance. Lockwood's account, lacking any overt narrator as it does, soon acquires the qualities of interiority, and revelation and we also satisfy our curiosity of reading someone's private papers dealing with strange things and people as well as his romance, which is a tendency widespread among mankind.

These things can be further clarified by comparing the fictional strategies employed in *Moll Flanders* and *Wuthering Heights* in regard to a subtle but very potent difference. In the preface to *Moll Flanders* an "I" takes the responsibility of presenting the heroine's autobiographical narrative after editing and desirable alterations: "the original of this story is put into new words, and the style of the famous lady we here speak of is a little altered, particularly she is made to tell her own tale in modester words than she told it at first, the copy which came first to hand having been written in language more like one still in Newgate than one grown penitent and humble, as she afterwards pretends to be." The writer of these lines certainly acts as a link between the story and the reader, and even inside her tale Moll tries to reach out to the reader as in the following apologia:

> With this stock I had the world to begin again; but you are to consider I was not now the same woman as when I lived at Rotherhithe.

There is an attempt in these devices to hook up the world of Moll Flanders with that of the reader and to provide a rational and realistic explanation for the telling of the story. Defoe employs the techniques of familiarisation to render a fantastic story credible. The situation of Lockwood's journal is at the opposite pole. It comes to our sight miraculously without any preliminaries and as our reading proceeds we become aware of a strange world whose facts and forces cannot be checked against our reality because they belong to a different plane of being. Defoe had sought to bring a fantastic tale within the compass of verisimilitude; Emily Brontë hurls into our eyes a reality raised to the nth degree where Heaven and Hell are conjoined, height and depth embrace each other, body and spirit melt together, good and evil present a mystical union, and the iron wall between life and death has disappeared.

D. **Complex Narrative Structure**

But the inside of the story is technically different: within the tale we find a complex system of narrative network. Viewed from outside the text is a closed work produced by Lockwood – the proper name itself may have been chosen for its suggestive value. Like Brontë children, he was, probably, in the habit of maintaining a journal, but more plausibly he has unwittingly led himself into a reality whose phenomena he finds worth recording; and pretty soon he develops an emotional involvement which impels him to carry forward his writing. In order to discover the antecedents of the strange people he has met he finds it convenient to take the help of Mrs. Nelly Dean, who happened to be quite familiar with the compounded history of the two houses: Wuthering Heights and Thrushcross Grange. So we find him recording the events as told by Mrs. Dean in her own words. And this introduces a dramatic element which is further developed, because Mrs. Dean herself prefers from time to time to reproduce for Lockwood the accounts offered by other characters. Several major and minor characters are given a chance to tell a part of the story where each is placed at a vantage point, that is, has the firsthand experience.

The resulting complexity is obvious as regards transmission of information, for example: Heathcliff to Mrs. Dean to Lockwood; Zillah to Mrs. Dean to Lockwood; Isabella to Mrs. Dean to Lockwood. Each person is allowed to present his or her own partial view of the reality and that is how this world goes: everyone interprets the reality in relation to himself. The author is absent; she will not presume to pass facile value judgments on a reality which is so baffling when one ponders it deeply. In this attitude she is like Homer, Chaucer and Shakespeare.

Each narrator describes situations and narrates events in which he or she personally took part or was present as an observer. Nelly Dean tends to reproduce rather than report the accounts given by another narrator. The narrators themselves reproduce the exchanges they had heard. This procedure confers some rare qualities on the novel; *Wuthering Heights* is perhaps the most vivid and dramatic tale written in English. The impression of the original account is maintained throughout with the result that when we hear Nelly Dean in the first person we tend to forget, for example, that it is Lockwood who is narrating what she told him, or when Zilla speaks, again modulating to the first person, we are too absorbed in her account to bother that it is Lockwood reproducing Nelly's reproduction of what Zillah told her. In this way, no matter how many layers of narration, the story always strikes us as freshly told.

Not all the narrators have the same status and there is no character in the novel who is there merely to tell part of the story. Even Zillah, the domestic servant, can produce a slight impact on the course of events, although quite negligible:

> She thinks Catherine haughty, and does not like her, I can guess by her talk. My young lady asked some aid of her when she first came; but Mr. Heathcliff told her to follow her own business, and let his daughter-in-law look after herself, and Zillah willingly acquiesced, being a narrow-minded selfish woman.

But Nelly Dean the main narrator, is different: she has a much bigger stature and has been given several functions. She is also an actor who influences the events as well as a chorus who comments on situations and characters, for, as we shall see later, she represents one of the value-scales involved in the moral scheme of the novel.

8. Narrative Modes

A. Reporting

Like the variety of narrators and sub-narrators, *Wuthering Heights* contains a rich variety of narrative modes. We have reporting by Lockwood in urbane economical racy language touched by light humour and wit as becomes an educated man:

> Joseph mumbled indistinctly in the depths of the cellar, but gave no intimation of ascending; so his master dived down to him, leaving me *vis-a-vis* the ruffianly bitch and a pair of grim shaggy sheep dogs, who shared with her a jealous guardianship over all my movements. Not anxious to come in contact with their fangs, I sat still; but imagining they would scarcely understand tacit insults, I

> unfortunately indulged in winking and making faces at the trio, and some turn of my physiognomy so irritated madam, that she suddenly broke into a fury, and leapt on my knees. I flung her back, and hastened to interpose the table between us. This proceeding roused the whole hive. Half-a-dozen four footed fiends, of various sizes and ages, issued from hidden dens to the common centre. I felt my heels and coat-laps peculiar subjects of assault; and, parrying off the larger combatants as effectually as I could with the poker, I was constrained to demand, aloud, assistance from some of the household in re-establishing peace.

Lockwood's reporting is also punctuated by his reflections on human nature and his own condition. This is quite natural in a man of his disposition, but these musings, as is to be expected, are brief and fall short of sustained philosophical thinking: "What vain weather-cocks we are!" And here is Nelly Dean reporting in her plain but engaging style, not omitting to mention the objects that touched her affections:

> Edgar Linton, as multitudes have been before and will be after him, was infatuated, and believed himself the happiest man alive on the day he led her to Gimmerton Chapel, three years subsequent to his father's death.
>
> Much against my inclination, I was persuaded to leave Wuthering Heights and accompany her here. Little Hareton was nearly five years old, and I had just begun to teach him his letters. We made a sad parting, but Catherine's tears were more powerful than ours. When I refused to go, and when she found her entreaties did not move me, she went lamenting to her husband and brother. The former offered me munificent wages; the latter ordered me to pack up – he wanted no women in the house, he said, now that there was no mistress, and as to Hareton, the curate should take him in hand, by and by. And so I had but one choice left: to do as I was ordered. I told master he got rid of all decent people only to run to ruin a little faster: I kissed Hareton good-bye; and since then he has been a stranger, and it's very queer to think it, but I have no doubt he has completely forgotten all about Ellen Dean, and

> that he was ever more than all the world to her, and she to him!

Where shall we find such 'feeling narration' that can stir our heart? – certainty not in the technically perfect objective narrator of modern fiction, who is dry as dust. Narration is the backbone of fiction and if it is without sap, how can the work be otherwise than pale and anaemic?

B. Description

As regards detailed description of persons and places, which has been a major convention of fiction writing, critics have commented on a noticeable lack of this mode in *Wuthering Heights*. In this regard, Emily Brontë stands apart from many major novelists. For most novelists pictorial representation is an essential requirement in creating a fictional character – it is believed to impart reality and life to the character. Take, for example, the following description in the opening chapter of *The Portrait of a Lady*:

> Tall, lean, loosely and feebly put together, he had an ugly, sickly, witty, charming face, furnished, but by no means decorated, with a straggling moustache and whisker. He looked clever and ill – a combination by no means felicitous, and he wore a brown velvet jacket. He carried his hands in his pockets, and there was something in the way he did it that showed the habit was inveterate. His gait had a shambling, wandering quality; he was not very firm on his legs.

Hardy's detailed and amusing "Description of Farmer Oak" in *Far From the Madding Crowd* is too well known to need any quotation. As to the places and landscape, Hardy's fiction offers some classic examples, but they are by no means absent elsewhere. George Eliot devoted one full chapter to the depiction of Dorlcote Mill and its background in *The Mill on the Floss*.

Compared to such impressive delineations, Emily Brontë's representations of people and places would appear sketchy, scattered, and poor. It is almost impossible to draw the face of even a leading character, not to talk of such persons as Nelly Dean and Hareton. And yet the wonder of it is that Emily Brontë's characters not only live, but they outlive themselves and re-live in our memory. Also just a few sentences about Wuthering Heights turn out to be as powerful and effective as any lengthy description of nature; the place undoubtedly has a haunting quality like a dark being.

Pragmatically speaking, therefore, we cannot lightly brush aside Emily Brontë's representations as deficient. The secret of her genius in this respect, perhaps, lies in a different technique. Her endeavour seems to be to characterise the essential being of each thing by dwelling only on those features that symbolise the dynamic core, or the spiritual self, if you like. She uncovers to us what Hopkins, drawing support from Duns Scotus's 'principle of individation', calls the 'inscape' of a thing: the *haecceitus* which makes the thing what it is, that which constitutes the unique being of a thing or person. And for this purpose she employs poetic rather than the usual fictional method of representation, which does not mean that she uses poetic prose everywhere, but that she resorts to images, condensation, syntactic manipulation and marked rhythm:

> She was the most winning thing that ever brought sunshine into a desolate house – a real beauty in face, with the Earnshaws' handsome dark eyes, but the Linton's fair skin, and small features, and yellow curling hair. Her spirit was high, though not rough, and qualified by a heart sensitive and lively to excess in its affections.

And here is the description of the landscape whose symbolic overtones point to the spirit of the place – mystical, sinister, desolate:

> ... the whole hill-back was one billowy, white ocean, the swells and falls not indicating corresponding rises and depressions in the ground; many pits, at least, were filled to a level; and entire ranges of mounds, the refuse of the quarries, blotted out from the chart which my yesterday's walk left pictured in my mind.

C. Dialogue

A prominent aspect of *Wuthering Heights* is the use of the dialogic mode. There are not many pages consisting entirely of reporting pure and simple. Generally in fiction reporting and dialogue alternate, but Emily Brontë has a powerful tendency to let dialogue preponderate and direct speech infiltrate into indirect narration. Here is one illustration of the latter:

> One of the maids mentioning the Fairy cave, quite turned

> her head with a desire to fulfil this project: She teased Mr. Linton about it; and he promised she should have the journey when she got older. But Miss Catherine measured her age by months, and, 'Now, am I old enough to go to Penistone Crags?' was the constant question in her mouth. The road thither would close by Wuthering Heights. Edgar had not the heart to pass it; so she received as constantly the answer, 'Not yet, love: not yet.'

And here's a crisp exchange:

> 'Why do you love him, Miss Cathy?
> 'Nonsense, I do – that's sufficient'.
> 'By no means; you must say why?'
> 'Well, because he is handsome, and pleasant to be with.'
> 'Bad!' was my commentary.
> 'And because he is young and cheerful'.
> 'Bad, still.'
> 'And because he loves me.'
> 'Indifferent, coming there.'

There are also instances of interior speech such as the following:

> 'Here we have the whole establishment of domestics, I suppose', was the reflection, suggested by this compound order. 'No wonder the grass grows up between the flags, and cattle are the only hedge-cutters.'

An extensive use of the dialogic or scenic mode brings certain advantages: it necessitates the use of the present tense in the direct speech portion and implies physical presence of the participants as well as situational properties. That means gain in immediacy and in dramatic quality. It endows the past events with concreteness and visual and aural clearness.

D. Epistolary Mode

There is even one instance of the epistolary mode and understandably it has raised many a critical eyebrow – the letter of Isabella addressed to Mrs. Dean. But the objection is sustainable only on a purely formal ground, and that too under the Jamesian view that the narrative point of view ought to be kept invariant. And even this charge can be met by pointing out that on a purely technical level, *Wuthering Heights* is a first person narrative from beginning to end, although within it there is a complex prismatic pattern of narrators and narrative modes. Moreover, technique in a novel cannot be evaluated *per se*: even direct authorial intrusion – indirectly the author is always present in his work – cannot be proscribed as always bad without any qualifications. It will therefore not be unwise to re-examine the point under discussion in the light of the following statement by Joseph Warran Beach.

> It is of course impossible to discuss novelistic technique without some regard for the subject-matter, the intentions, of the writer considered. For obviously the object of the technique is to help realise the artistic intention, and we shall see over and over again how the specific effect sought by the artist determines the technical methods consciously or unconsciously chosen.
>
> (*The Twentieth Century Novel*)

Now one of the intentions clearly discernible within the text itself is to mark the degradation of Heathcliff and poisoning of life along one of the moral scales (more than one and contradictory moral scales are invoked in the novel). Each point in this process (downward and upward progress simultaneously) is sought to be distinguished by using some device – poetical, synthetic, structural or discoursal. In the brutalisation of life through Heathcliff a stage is reached when doubts begin to appear as to whether Heathcliff is human at all – he may be mad, or he may be a demon. And this is precisely the burden of Isabella's letter which has the other function of filling the gap in Mrs. Dean's narrative. The device of the letter which stands out clearly in the narrative of a different mode achieves the purpose of foregrounding the aforementioned stage in the moral scheme of the story: Isabella, who, unlike our narrator Mrs. Dean, is a direct victim of Heathcliff's inhumanity, relates what she suffered in a kind of communication that is meant for disclosing what is in one's heart.

There is a further point also. When we apply the criterion of probability, the writing of the letter by Isabella appears to be the most likely – if not the only – choice open to her. Her explanation is quite convincing:

> I came last night to Wuthering Heights, and heard, for the first time, that Catherine has been and is yet, very ill. I must not write to her, I suppose, and my brother is either too angry or too distressed to answer what I send him. Still, I must write to somebody, and the only choice left to me is you.

9. Criticism

Although most writers have found the narrative in *Wuthering Heights* impeccable and faultless, there are certain things which can be mentioned by way of criticism. An extreme view is that of Patterson, who in his biographical article on the Brontës (*Six Centuries of English Literature V*) finds *Wuthering Heights* "badly constructed", but this is certainly a minority opinion which most critics would consider harsh and unperceptive. Patterson, however concedes that the work has a strong appeal for many readers and that "its truth is the truth of poetry, not of romance". Bonamy Dobree's statement in his introduction to the novel is more specific and, perhaps, not to be dismissed so easily, although with regard to the epistolary device we have already found the choice defensible. Dobree writes:

> What, we ask, was the 'good authority' which apprised Dr. Kenneth of there being something afoot between Heathcliff and Isabella? And how, soon afterwards, did Nelly Dean get Isabella's letter, and why was such an unlikely epistle addressed to her at all?

But he hastens to add quite significantly:

> Just for a moment, then, the pressure slackens: but it is for a moment only that we feel uneasiness. Such is the force and passion of the prose, the speed of the narrative, that we soon accept again.

He also finds the verbatime reporting somewhat clumsy; and it is true that each narrator is made to perform the unbelievable feat of reproducing long stretches of dialogue. For example, Zillah repeats what she heard to Mrs. Dean, Mrs. Dean reproduces it to Lockwood and Lockwood records everything he got from Mrs. Dean. The whole concatenation is not only clumsy, it requires an unusually photographic memory.

But all this granted, the net result of this procedure is simply brilliant in terms of dramatic quality and immediacy which are hard to find elsewhere in English fiction.

10. Time Scales

Emily Brontë's skilful management of a double time scale

constitutes an outstanding feat in the history of novelistic form. There is nothing in the fiction of the last century to compare with her bold experiment and achievement – Lockwood's journal opens when only two turns of the screw are left: Heathcliff's death and re-establishment of human balance and value, gaiety, love and aesthetic urge.

The two time-scales employed in the novel keep converging at certain points and this makes the past and present mingle in such a way that the whole experience of the novel strikes the reader with great immediacy, in spite of two, and on occasions three, mediators. Lockwood's clock begins to tick in the cold season of 1801. He has rented Thrushcross Grange in order to spend one year away from the human company. Soon after arriving, he pays a visit to his landlord at Wuthering Heights and immediately after returning from there he begins writing his experience. He met Heathcliff and found him a peculiarly unsocial person. We get a description of the house and its surroundings and are also made aware of its symbolic meaning. Lockwood also records how he was attacked by a pack of dogs kept in the house.

Lockwood pays a second visit to Wuthering Heights and is met with greater unwelcomeness. He finds Mrs. Heathcliff attractive but uncivil and Hareton a mere rustic, and he makes mistakes as regards their identity within the family. Angered by an insulting remark of Heathcliff, Lockwood rushes out snatching a lantern from Joseph, who immediately sets the dogs on him. Lockwood is unharmed but badly shaken. His plight provides occasion for merriment to Heathcliff and Hareton, but the master of the house relents and allows him to pass the night under his roof.

The good servant Zillah conducts the visitor to an uninhabited room where he discovers Catherine's journal and reads a part of it without getting a sound sleep. Lockwood sees two bad dreams, and the second dream about Catherine is so intense that he is unable to judge whether it is a nightmare or ghostly reality. He is so frightened and immobilised that he makes a terrible sound. Heathcliff is awakened; he rushes in, but his strange behaviour and ejaculations further deepen the awe and mystery instead of mitigating them. In the early morning Lockwood left the Heights and Heathcliff, on second thoughts, gave him company up to the gate of Thrushcross park.

These two visits' experience delivered directly by Lockwood fills his mind with so much curiosity and also a shy desire, as indicated earlier – that he calls the housekeeper Mrs. Dean and solicits her to reveal the past of Mr. Heathcliff and his family, which is so tantalising to him (and to the reader). At this point, the second time-scale is activised. This clock takes us backwards by thirty years around the year 1771, when Heathcliff was brought to Earnshaw home at Wuthering Heights. The two times start moving concurrently, but at varying paces; during the period of short units of time in which Nelly is telling the story, the story itself is moving forward – the future is creeping nearer, its edge is continuously converted into the 'present' and the present itself melts into the past.

Mrs. Dean's account proceeds chronologically to the evening when the Lintons are on a visit to Wuthering Heights and Heathcliff has been humiliated before everybody and kept out of the dinner and dance party. She interrupts herself at a very suspenseful point after reporting this exchange between Heathcliff and herself:

> 'I' m trying to settle how I shall pay Hindley back. I don't care how long I wait, if I can only do it at last. I hope he will not die before I do!' 'For shame, Heathcliff!' said I. 'It is for God to punish wicked people; we should learn to forgive.' 'No, God won't have the satisfaction that I shall,' he returned. I only wish I knew the best way! Let me alone, and I'll plan it out: while I'm thinking of that I don't feel pain.'

Mrs. Dean turns to Lockwood and we are called back to the 'present'. The conversation that takes place between the two again tells us how the novel should be read. After praising Mrs. Dean's method of narration, Lockwood implores her not to "leap over some three years", as she wanted, saying:

> 'Are you acquainted with the mood of mind in which if you were seated alone and the cat licking its kitten on the rug before you, you would watch the operation so intently that the puss's neglect of one ear would put you seriously out of temper?

The second clock is re-started with the summer of 1778: "On the morning of a fine June day, my first bonny little nursling, and the last of the ancient Earnshaw stock, was born." This instalment takes us to 1783, the year in which Catherine got married to Edgar Linton (Heathcliff had disappeared before that) and Nelly had to accompany her to Thrushcross Grange, and the memory of parting from Hareton brings her to the present: he has been a stranger to her up to 'now', that is 1801.

When the journal is resumed, we are still in the 'present': we learn that Lockwood, as he had feared, has been ill for four weeks. Presumably hearing of his sickness, Heathcliff came to see him a short while earlier; seven days before, he had sent him a brace of grouse. Lockwood is still quite weak; he calls Mrs. Dean and requests her to finish the story. We are swung back to the past. Heathcliff had returned after three years' absence and had immediately put his plan of revenge into operation including his marriage with Isabella. When Mrs. Dean went to Wuthering Heights in response to Isabella's distressed call, she was forced by Heathcliff to carry his letter to Catherine. At this point Mr. Kenneth arrives and the story is interrupted. Lockwood records that the history being related by Mrs. Dean is "dree and dreary", not the kind of thing he should have chosen to amuse himself, but he will extract something good out of it. He then looks at the picture of younger Catherine and writes: ".... let me beware of the fascination that lurks in Catherine Heathcliff's brilliant eyes. I should be in a curious taking if I surrendered my heart to that young person, and the daughter turned out a second edition of the mother."

When Lockwood sits down again at the writing table, several days have passed. During this period he has heard the whole history of the two houses, at different sittings. This means the story has been brought up to date, but not all of it has been recorded. This means Lockwood now possesses the knowledge of all the happenings up to the time of his illness, including Catherine Heathcliff's birth, marriage and widowhood : hence his reflection about her charm. He now decides to write down the remaining part of the story that he has heard, with minor editing: "I'll continue it in her own words, only a little condensed. She is, on the whole, a very fair narrator, and I don't think I could improve her style."

We go back to the past to pick up the thread of the story a little condensed and recorded by Lockwood. Mrs. Dean continues to be the narrator, but what tends to be overlooked in Lockwood's reproduction is that he does not expunge the dialogues which took place between himself and Nelly or where she employed the second person pronoun. These portions create an illusion of the intruding present, but that is not so. For example, when Lockwood records the clause "At about twelve o' clock that night, was born the Catherine you saw at Wuthering Heights", he means that this is what Nelly said, when she was telling the remaining part of the story. The same thing applies to the opening dialogue in chapter 25.

The first clock concerned with Lockwood's direct experience begin to be heard again at the end of Chapter 30:

> Thus ended Mrs. Dean's story. Notwithstanding the doctor's prophecy, I am rapidly recovering strength, and, though it be only the second week in January, I propose getting out on horseback in a day or two, and riding over to Wuthering Heights, to inform my landlord that I shall spend the next six months in London; and if he likes, he may look out for another tenant to take the place, after October I would not pass another winter here for much.

In the next chapter Lockwood becomes a minor participant and a direct witness to the events; the two time scales mingle and run simultaneously. Lockwood journeys to Wuthering Heights to inform Heathcliff of his change of mind; he also carries Nelly's letter to Cathy which he somehow manages to deliver. The longer time scale also moves a little and the story advances by two small but significant steps. Behind the apparent quarrel between Cathy and Hareton that takes place in front of Lockwood, there is perceptible a softening on both sides; and secondly Heathcliff's grim resolve to ruin the progeny of his dead adversaries betrays signs of weakening. As Hareton left the room, Heathcliff looked hard at him and sighed; "It would be odd, if I thwart myself'! he muttered."

The next entry in the journal is dated simply 1802. It must have been written after September when Lockwood made a flying visit to Thrushcross Grange and then to Wuthering Heights. During the period that Lockwood has been absent from the scene, history has taken two giant steps: part of one of the reversals is directly noted and recorded by Lockwood, not without a slight feeling of jealousy – this is the reconciliation of the young people; and the second, namely, the strange end of Heathcliff, is related to him by Mrs. Dean within the longer time scale. But the novel ends with focus on Lockwood's final experience and not with Mrs. Dean's reporting -- and thus within the shorter time-scale Wuthering Heights purports to be an account of a compact, staggering experience of Lockwood constituted of what he witnessed, felt and heard.

11. Moral Scales

Emily Brontë's use of the moral framework is no less powerful and profound. It consists of a triangle of value systems surrounding the inexplicable grand passion of Catherine and Heathcliff which defies them all. There is also a fifth scale which emerges and triumphs as a wholesome outcome of the warring systems.

The three framing systems are represented by Lockwood, Mrs. Dean and Joseph. The first is the norm of the civilised society going no deeper than polite behaviour and decency. The second is characterised by practical good sense and common Christian morality. The third is marked by fanaticism, hypocrisy, and superstition. These systems become operative from the beginning in a criticising role and the remarks of their mouthpieces in respect of the central mighty passion of Heathcliff and Catherine individually suggest that Emily Brontë meant them to be taken in that light. Although, of necessity, Lockwood's values remain suspended for a major portion of the novel simply because he wasn't there; still, such remarks as the following, already quoted in another context, make his attitude quite clear:

> ... let me beware of the fascination that lurks in Catherine Heathcliff's brilliant eyes. I should be in a curious taking if I surrendered my heart to that young person, and the daughter turned out a second edition of the mother.

This mechanism of colliding value-scales sets up a fine superstructure of auto-criticism in the novel in which the extremism, complete amorality and impracticability of Heathcliff-Catherine relationship – the central theme – are exposed at every step by the three opposing systems which find it difficult to sustain its vigorous onslaught. On the other hand, the self-sustaining torrential natural 'morality' which informs the very being of Heathcliff and Catherine, batters and bruises the contending forces and drags to light their weaknesses: shallowness, narrowness, hypocrisy, etc, etc.

In the midst of this strife on the moral plane, when these fighting forces are getting exhausted, there arises the sensible, joyful human love of Hareton and Cathy. It is in keeping with the Christian spirit that this value-system should emerge out of suffering – penance – and should be in the nature of a recognition or discovery. It is not so impressive as the blinding passion of Heathcliff and Catherine, but it is distinctively human, and healthy and gay, and constructive – the best thing that humanity can aspire to have this side of death.

12. Poetic Quality

Already we have come very close to another prominent feature of *Wuthering Heights*, namely its poetry. *Wuthering Heights* is conceived in the intensest heat of poetic inspiration and it takes us to a dizzy height on the mount of the Muses. The poetic intentions and the symbolic design become clear from the outset: the place-symbolises that harsh unrelenting force of the cosmos which brings forth and purges ("destroyer and preserver") the evil in human nature; 'Wuthering Heights', as its two components connote takes the soul to that elevated point of terrific motions, where it is frightened and unhinged and loses the distinction between good and evil; it passes through the "dark night" as conceived in Christian mysticism, though the experience in the novel is objectified as in drama. The novel is more satisfying than a negative poem like *The Waste Land* since it takes the soul beyond 'the Valley of the Sadow of Death' to the country of the Beulah from where we have a glimpse of the light (not in the strict Christian sense, though it may be in the background) and love and beauty of human life.

It would be wrong to assume that the last part of the book depicting the happiness of Hareton and Cathy in one another and in nature is a sentimental, addendum which compromises Emily's art and weakens it. Far from it, the visible promise of bliss is part of the structure of an unfrustrated mystical experience, and *Wuthering Heights* is an allegory of that experience.

"Its truth is the truth of poetry" admitted Patterson; and to tell the whole truth about *Wuthering Heights*, it must be added that the tree of love in this work brings forth two fruits: one palpable and human; and the other in the other world whose true nature is unknown–perhaps, unknowable.

To continue with the symbolism of the places, Thrushcross Grange represents the metaphysical principle of calm and the main drama of the action involves the clash and resolution of the two cosmic forces, designated by David Cecil as the Principle of Storm and the Principle of Calm. Like Wuthering Heights, as explained earlier, Thrushcross Grange creates the aroma of its own spirit through the symbolic overtones of its name, situation, natural ambience and occupants.

There is also another paradigm on which the poetic structure and the deep meaning arising out of it can be studied; this is imagery, or, more properly, 'imaginative field'. Elizabeth Th. Van De Laar has produced an impressive analysis of the imagery of *Wuthering Heights*, pleading that this is the inner structure of the novel: significantly she called her book, *The Inner Structure* of *Wuthering Heights: A Study of an Imaginative Field*.

Literary imagination, it is assumed, is the organising principle of a literary work of art and images are regarded as the verbal expression of the literary imagination. Explaining the idea of 'inner structure' De Laar observes:

> ... the inner structure will be seen as the pattern made by the literary imagination, *i.e.* by that spiritual mobility which is characterised by the ability to transform sights and sounds, forms and colours, suggested by perception or memory, into a new sequence of living images which has the power to open up new worlds of experience and thereby to enrich the language.

De Laar then proceeds to describe and analyse the images employed in respect of each character under ten heads; these categories are: air; water; earth; fire; weather; dreams, visions, forebodings, premonitions, omens; windows, doors, keys, walls, gates, mirrors, portraits; animal and vegetable life; books, the Bible; light and darkness. The results of this detailed study are quite revealing although De Laar's interpretation may not evoke unanimous acceptance.

Catherine is strongly associated with the element of air, specially in its more violent aspects. The Imagery of air related to Heathcliff is focused on violent wind and "the dynamism of height and storm forms the symbolic pattern of his life." A significant difference noted between Catherine and Heathcliff is that the latter is steeped in darkness unredeemed whereas Catherine in her last illness longs for light: "I am wearying to escape into that glorious world, and to be always there."

De Laar's final statement of the essence of the novel, or its poetic centre, is certainly very impressive:

> Out of the primordial darkness with its potentialities of procreation arose the light, and the light generated life. Emily Brontë's novel culminates in the negation of light: she creates "life in darkness" a form of life which may seem inconceivable, and even abhorrent, though its

mysterious power will continue to intrigue and fascinate. "Life in darkness": this examination – which might perhaps be considered as just one aid to the understanding of a great novel – has revealed this to be the epitome of *Wuthering Heights*.

De Laar's work unmistakably points to a fundamental dimension of *Wuthering Heights*; namely, its poetic nature: that is to say, Emily Brontë is unique among the nineteenth century novelists in conceiving and executing her story as a poem – a dramatic poem. She writes in terms of symbols and images; presents dramatic scenes and vivid pictorial descriptions; aims at condensation rather than exegesis; provides a double structure to the tale; concerns herself with the basic and universal issues of life (and death); and carefully selects words and sentences which build poetic rhythms and cadences.

Like De Laar, G.D. Klingopulos has discussed *Wuthering Heights* from the poetic point of view: it is one of those novels that are best regarded as dramatic poems. This novel demands the same kind of reading as Macbeth:

> If *Wuthering Heights* does not represent the coherence of a *Macbeth*, it is important to remember that the novel is the first in English which invites the same kind of attention that we give to *Macbeth*. It has a similar complexity, makes the same claim as poetry.

Not that the nineteenth-century fiction is altogether devoid of poetic passages: as David Cecil has remarked Charlotte Brontë and Dickens, for example, frequently rise to poetic fervour in their handling of atmosphere and mood, respectively. But what distinguishes Emily Brontë is that poetry is intrinsic to her plan and that when inspiration is at its fullest charge she "rises to poetry of a rarer kind." As an example, one might ponder the following passage from Catherine's manic outpouring, which is part of a larger portion quoted by Cecil:

> " 'That's a turkey's', she murmured to herself; 'and this is a wild duck's; and this is a pigeon's. Ah, they put pigeon's feathers in the pillows – no wonder I couldn't die! Let me take care to throw it on the floor when I lie down. And there is a moor-cock's; and this – I should know it among a thousand – it's a lapwing's. Bonny bird; wheeling over our heads in the middle of the moor. It wanted to get to

> its nest, for the clouds had touched the swells, and it felt rain coming. This feather was picked up from the heath, the bird was not shot; we saw its nest in the winter, full of little skeletons. Heathcliff set a trap over it, and the old ones dared not come. I made him promise he'd never shoot a lapwing after that, and he didn't. Yes here are more! Did he shoot my lapwings, Nelly? Are they red, any of them? Let me look."

Where shall we find such poetry outside *King Lear* or *Macbeth*? This is a unified beautiful poem with a riotous display of visual and tactile (implied) images in finely patterned diction and syntax. More than that, it has a profoundly moving poetic theme encompassing nature's beauty and innocence, man's transgression and sin, expiation and the final doubt.

Wuthering Heights is replete with lyrical utterances, long and short, coming from Heathcliff, Catherine and Cathy. And it is illuminated by true purple passages which unerringly combine poetic inspiration with superb craftsmanship. One such passage is Heathcliff's description of the interior of Thrushcross Grange drawing room. It is only natural that the boy Heathcliff, who had been painfully made conscious of his swarthiness, should be tantalised by colour and hue:

> The light came from thence; they had not put up the shutters, and the curtains were only half closed. Both of us were able to look in by standing on the basement and clinging to the ledge, and we saw - ah! it was beautiful – a splendid place carpeted with crimson, and crimson-covered chairs and tables, and a pure white ceiling bordered by gold, a shower of glass-drops hanging in silver chairs from the centre and shimmering with little soft tapers.

Even greater – perhaps the greatest poetry ever written in prose form – is to be found in Cathy's description of Linton's and her own idea of bliss – a piece of writing which, when closely studied, will turn out to be a marvel of poetic craftsmanship in its texture and design:

> He said the pleasantest manner of spending a hot July day was lying from morning till evening on a bank of heath in the middle of the moors, with the bees humming dreamily about among the bloom, and the larks singing high up overhead, and the blue sky and bright sun shining steadily

> and cloudlessly. That was his most perfect idea of heaven's happiness; mine was rocking in a rustling green tree, with west wind blowing, and bright white clouds flitting rapidly above; and not only larks, but throstles, and blackbirds, and linnets, and cuckoos pouring out music on every side, and the moors seen at a distance, broken into cool dusky dells; but close by great swells of long grass undulating in waves to the breeze; and woods and sounding water, and the whole world awake and wild with joy. He wanted all to lie in an ecstasy of peace; I wanted all to sparkle and dance in a glorious jubilee.

The two visions of contrasting states are neatly separated by a short comment in the middle of the passage: "That was his most perfect idea of heaven's happiness; mine was...." The structure of each description is so intricate that it is a challenge to the analyst. Alliteration and sound-patterning are so integral to the music of the two sections that they are not perceived as contrived or imposed. Each word seems to be carefully weighed for its appropriate effect in terms of its form, sound, meaning and connotation. Even the various inflections of words, conjunctions and pauses of different durations, are exactly the right ones for the desired mood, *e.g.* in "I wanted all to sparkle, and dance in a glorious jubilee" – the effect would be different if there were no pause in the middle of the sentence.

The employment of imagery is superb. The main appeal is to the images of sight, sound and motion, but the imagery in Linton's vision is in contrast with that of Cathy. The images in the first part are differentiated from those of the second part in terms of visual strength, magnitude and speed. The sequencing of images is also not random; it follows a subtle artistic design.

In the foregoing discussion, an attempt has been made to define and clarify Emily's poetic intentions and poetic art that governed the composition of *Wuthering Heights* (in fact, she deserves credit for something even greater: her combining of a profound poetic vision with realism). Truly speaking, the novel is in continuation of and of a piece with her poetic perceptions.

In "last Lines", the poet declares that her soul is not cowardly; she is able to face "the world's storm-troubled sphere". She penetrated to the mystery of life where she saw energies of the cosmos moulding the nature of man, but she also saw evolution in spiritual terms:

With wide-embracing love
Thy spirit animates eternal years,
Pervades and broods above,
Changes, sustains, dissolves, creates, and rears.

She is firmly anchored on "the steadfast rock of immortality and finds no room for Death / Nor atom that his might could render void." The lonely mountains reveal to her "more glory and more grief" than she can tell; and the human heart which is awakened to feeling by nature can perceive the essential truth of "both the worlds of Heaven and Hell" (Stanzas).

13. The Question of Tradition

When we focus on the poetic aspect of *Wuthering Heights*, we find Emily Brontë closer to Blake and Shakespeare of *King Lear* than to any English novelist. And this raises the question of her place in the British literary tradition. It is to this problem that we shall now turn our attention. We shall take for our point of departure the following brief – rather equivocal – remarks of F.R. Leavis in *The Great Tradition*:

> I have said nothing about *Wuthering Heights* because that astonishing work seems to me a kind of sport. It may, all the same, very well have had some influence of an essentially undetectable kind: she broke completely, and in the most challenging way, both with the Scott tradition that imposed on the novelist a romantic resolution of his theme, and with the tradition coming down from the eighteenth century that demanded a plane-mirror reflection of the surface of 'real' life. Out of her a minor tradition comes, to which belongs most notably, *The House of the Green Shutters*.

"A kind of sport" seems to be quite a pregnant phrase, but the author forbears to deliver its full meaning; Is it a product of fancy, an experiment in form, or a serious affair of the human soul? – nothing is made clear. We are told what Emily Brontë avoided and not what she embraced and contributed. The difficulty created by this phrase is obvious from the way it is referred to by Walter Allen:

> F.R. Leavis in *The Great Tradition* has called it a sport. Therein lies the primary difficulty in dealing with it. It is utterly unlike any other novel. There is nothing one can compare it to, for the great masters of form have chosen

> subjects so different from it as to make *Wuthering Heights* exist in a category of creation all its own.
>
> (*The English Novel*)

Allen's own difficulty is indicated by the way he is seeking to interpret the overloaded (or is it partly empty?) term.

A further complication is created by Leavis's definition of 'the great tradition': he means by it "the tradition to which what is great in English fiction belongs" – Jane Austen is regarded as the inaugurator of the great tradition and its great luminaries are George Eliot, Henry James and Conrad. These great novelists of English are distinguished by their keen concern with form, but they are no mere aesthetes, for their other necessary attribute is moral preoccupation. Now if these are Mr. Leavis's qualifying terms for a great novelist one wonders how Emily Brontë can be kept outside the list. As regards greatness, there is hardly any writer on *Wuthering Heights* who has not used the term 'great', or some other expression meaning the same thing in his evaluation of the novel. In fact, 'unique' and 'great' – these two words have been so widely used for the novel that it would be purely gratuitous to support the point by quoting from critics. Therefore, if we go by the majority view and not rely on Leavis as the only authority to pronounce on the matter, Emily Brontë's novel is undoubtedly a great novel and hence an important work within the great tradition.

Wuthering Heights does not fall short of Leavis's other criteria also. As has been adequately dealt with earlier, Emily Brontë is a great innovator in novelistic form and her novel is flawless; not only that: in matters of plot construction, use of narrative devices, management of the time scales and absence of the author from the world of the novel, she is definitely a precursor of the moderns – and also, one might add, in infusing poetry into a realistic story. Whether the moderns consciously took advantage of her achievements or not is another matter, but there is no doubt that the development of the novel in the twentieth century has been largely along the lines drawn by Emily Brontë.

Coming to the question of moral preoccupation, it needs only to be reiterated that the basic theme of *Wuthering Heights* is the problem of evil in the sense in which the mystics struggle to comprehend it: it does not offer any facile solution nor does it bow to the conventional view of good and evil: it is the story of love wounded and healed.

But even if these pleas are accepted by Mr. Leavis, he will still be unable to admit Emily Brontë to the great tradition because she is too big to be confined within the limits of his conception; in other words, she requires a different and a much broader idea of tradition. Perhaps Eliot, who, in his poetry, drew sustenance from the whole field of European literature without regard to the genre-boundaries can turn out to be a better guide, at least in certain respects.

Eliot's essay "Tradition and the Individual Talent" has more than one weakness: it has a misleading ring of novelty, it is ambiguous at many places and suffers from fallaciousness; but our aim is not to vouch for the soundness of everything said there; we shall be concerned only with certain ideas which are least susceptible to controversy.

For Eliot, tradition for the Western writer is constituted by the European literature of the past, felt by the writer as a still living and moulding force. What he calls "the historical sense" compels a man

> to write not merely with his own generation in his bones, but with a feeling that the whole of the literature of Europe from Homer and within it the whole of the literature of his own country has a simultaneous existence and composes a simultaneous order.

This conception of tradition at first sight seems to require an encyclopaedic knowledge, but from Eliot's own explanation it can be reasonably deduced that what he wants the writer to do is to have the capacity to feel and grasp the essence of past writing rather than memorize every bit and piece of it:

> Some can absorb knowledge, the more tardy must sweat for it, Shakespeare acquired more essential history from Plutarch than most men could from the whole British Museum.

This widened view of tradition and of the way in which it should be absorbed is not only desirable but also necessary if we wish to give a satisfactory account of the best that has been written in modern English fiction with its adoption of the modes and methods of the other genres — drama and poetry. How can we really accommodate the best of Conrad, Virginia Woolf, James Joyce and D.H. Lawrence within the narrow limits of Leavis's "great tradition"? We shall see that Emily Brontë, like the above writers, is too big for Leavis's receptacle which has neither the requisite width nor depth.

There are two other points to be discussed before we can delineate Emily Brontë's relation to the tradition. The first is the application of the term 'unique' to *Wuthering Heights* with a somewhat misleading elaboration. Its admiring commentators have asserted with great zeal that there is nothing like it in the whole realm of English fiction, even the entire literature; meaning that the work is purely a result of the author's afflatus, woven, like a spider's web, out of her own nature and experience of life on the moors. *Wuthering Heights* as Charlotte Brontë assures us in her Preface "was hewn in a wild workshop, with simple tools, out of homely materials".

According to T.S. Eliot, there is a general tendency among readers and critics to dwell on the most individual aspects of a poet's work, and this results in suppressing his links with the poet:

> One of the facts that might come to light.... is our tendency to insist, when we praise a poet upon those aspects of his work in which he least resembles anyone else. In these aspects or parts of his work we pretend to find what is individual, what is the peculiar essence of the man. We dwell with satisfaction upon the poet's difference from his predecessors, especially his immediate predecessors; we endeavour to find something that can be isolated in order to be enjoyed. Whereas if we approach a poet without this prejudice we shall often find that not only the best but the most individual parts of his work may be those in which the dead poets, his ancestors assert their immortality most vigorously.

Eliot is, perhaps, overstating his case, but the obvious fact remains – and a close study will reveal it – that the best writers of the world owe their greatness not to presenting something quite new, but to transforming what they got from their predecessors into something new and strange – and it is only in this sense that their work is unique.

Secondly, Eliot in "Tradition and the Individual Talent" (from which we have been quoting) suggests that tradition involves sacrifice of personal emotion in favour of impersonality. The form in which Eliot has explained his theory of impersonality makes it baffling and unacceptable: How can a writer eschew emotion altogether in order to express it in art? Is there absolutely no connection between jealousy as experienced by Shakespeare and as presented in his plays?

We shall not concern ourselves with this and other problems.

What is of importance here is Eliot's hint that in order to become an aesthetic object and an object of the tradition, the poet's experience must undergo depersonalisation – and in this there is nothing new except that for a work of art to be a part of the tradition the experience therein must stand independently with self validation and its own structure.

Now to take the last point first, *Wuthering Heights* is a self-supporting work in which the author has consumed her personality entirely; the timeless beauty of the passion with attendant and consequent patterns of life is not at all besmirched by the mundane reality of her life. This does not mean that there is no message, but the message encoded properly as a product of the author's imagination has become a public object. Since in another context, we have already dealt with this aspect of *Wuthering Heights*, let us move on to the main question of Emily Brontë's relation to the tradition and the magnitude of that tradition. Both these facets of the question can be properly taken care of by exploring the sources of *Wuthering Heights*, both thematic and formal.

Emily's father, Patrick Brontë, had been a bright scholar who opened a public school at the age of sixteen and at twentyfive proceeded to Cambridge where he studied for four years for his degree. His library at the parsonage of Haworth provided no mean stuff for reading: it contained the works of all the major English poets. The children, left to their own resources in a lonely place must have read again and again the entire collection. The romantic worlds of Gondal and Angria raised by them with meticulous attention to detail bear unmistakable marks of Walter Scott's poetry and novels. The world of *Wuthering Heights*, though much more substantial and realistic, also shows signs of Scott's influence, but its human composition is far more complex. Scott's world is compounded with Byron's hero. Then there are clear echoes of Shakespeare's tragedies, the Bible and other religious literature – and these, as we know, are some of the major elements of the British literary tradition. The structure of the mystical passages and the conception of good and evil in the novel are so close to Blake's thinking that they cannot be regarded as the result of mere coincidence.

Already we have crossed the narrow limits of Leavis's great tradition. In order to find its proper place in English literature, we must try to place *Wuthering Heights* within the broad tradition composed of poetry, novel and drama. Not only in theme and feeling but in language and form as well, this novel stands astride of the three genres. But that is not all.

A major influence, and a formative influence, is that of the medieval balladry with its graveyards, haunted places and ghosts and premonitions – and tragic loves. Cathy one day caught Hareton reading "Chevy Chase" in an execrable manner – "Chevy Chose" which had been one of her favourite pieces. In chapter 31, we learn that Cathy possessed a rich hoard of books (which she recalls with deep feeling) before Heathcliff resolved to destroy it; what remained had been pilfered by Hareton:

> "I was always reading, when I had them" said Catherine, "and Mr. Heathcliff never reads; so he took it into his head to destroy my books. I have not had a glimpse of one for weeks. Only once, I searched through Joseph's store of theology, to his great irritation; and once Hareton, I came upon a secret stock in your room.... some Latin and Greek, and some tales and poetry, all old friends – I brought the last here – and you gathered them as a magpie gathers silver spoons, for the mere love of stealing......
> But I've most of them written on my brain and printed in my heart, and you cannot deprive me of those."

There is even a close parallel between *Wuthering Heights* and the well-known ballad called "The Demon Lover" of which more than 145 versions have been collected. The kernel of the story is the carrying away of a woman by the ghost of her lover. The ballad, as ballads do, plunges the readers into the middle of the action:

> 'O whare hae ya been, my dearest dear,
> These seven lang years and more?'
> 'O I am come to seek my former vows
> That ye promised me before.'

and ends on a sinister note:

> He's tane her by the milk-white hand
> And he's thrown her in the main;
> And full five and twenty hundred ships
> Perished all on the coast of Spain,

Heathcliff's resolve to lie by the side of Catherine after his death reminds us of Margaret's cry to her dead lover whose spirit has guided her to his grave:

> 'Is there any room at your head, Saunders
> Is there any room at your feet?

Or any room at your side, Saunders,
Where fain, fain, I wad asleep?'
("Clerk Saunders")

In the same connection, we have to mention what Winifred Gerin calls Emily's German studies. The reference is to a series of articles on the poems and ballads of Schiller by Bulwar Lytton which appeared in *Blackwood's Magazine* from September 1842 to August 1843. These articles included substantial portions of Schiller's poetry in translation. Gerin observes that "the poetry of Schiller, with its ballad form and fiery substance, held obvious attraction for Emily".

This would seem to take us beyond the native sources, and we must begin thinking in terms of the European tradition, however slight or indirect the contact might have been. There is also another German source to be taken into account, namely, the romantic writer, Hoffman's novel, *Devil's Elixir (Elixire des Teufels)* dealing with the motif of a doppelganger. In a review of the novel printed in *Blackwood's*, the writer noted Hoffmann's contribution to the novel of evil possession and Gerin adds "it was this notion that James Hogg used to such telling effect in his *Confessions of a Justified Sinner*".

It is necessary to emphasize at this point that Emily took the idea of evil possession only to transform it and put it to a new use. In *Wuthering Heights*, it is refined to a form in which it stands delicately poised between demonism and psychological realism with a tilt towards the latter, with the result that it appears unlikely that the person who returns after an absence of three years is not real Heathcliff, but his wicked double, or an evil spirit, or his ghost, who has come to fetch Catherine to the nether world.

Heathcliff is very different from Hoffman's Capuchin monk after taking the mysterious portion and Hogg's Robert Wringhim after coming under the spell of his evil genius. Heathcliff does not commit gruesome murders; he keeps a warm house well supplied with food and drinks. He does perform with particular relish the rites of cruelty, but they are explainable in terms of his rather excessive reaction to the torture and humiliation he had undergone during his malleable years. He even conceals behind his inhuman conduct an affection for Hareton and Cathy, which his hatred cannot wipe out completely: he 'sees' the signs of Catherine in their figures.

But, the ambiguity about Heathcliff's true nature is never abandoned till the end. And the skill with which this ambiguity is maintained points to a deeper purpose: a groping towards the ultimate mystery of good and evil.

To the Gothic or horror novel, Emily Brontë stands in a special relationship. The Gothic fiction itself in its broadened scope constitutes an important strand in the tradition with writers of talent such as Walpole, Anne Radcliffe, Mary Shelley and Poe in its fold – even Henry James and Faulkener exploited the Gothic element in some of their works. Since Walpole published his *Castle of Otranto* in 1764, the Gothic novel has been constantly growing and changing and even in the twentieth century the tradition is continued though the horrors are of a different kind and of a different origin.

Emily Brontë and Henry James made remarkable contributions to this sub-genre; and what has been said about *The Turn of the Screw* can, with some modification, be applied to *Wuthering Heights*: James's story, "is much more than a ghost story"; Emily's novel is much more than a horror story. The first thing that she achieved was the domestication of the Gothic novel: she gave it a local habitation and a name, planting the uncanny machinery firmly into the English landscape and English life, and yet retaining a trace of it in the doubtful ancestry of the hero. As Gerin observes, "It is perhaps the quality of nearness that she brought to the world of the Gothic novel that is her major contribution to the genre." Secondly, she left open the way for a psychological explanation of the unnatural and abnormal occurrences. But in spite of this empirical convincingness as well as domestication, Emily Brontë powerfully makes us feel that there is a life beyond death, that there is an inscrutable mystery at the centre of things and good and evil can have no apt definition – she shows us "fear in a handful of dust", which is a superior kind of the Gothic effect.

The foregoing discussion was undertaken with a view to revealing Emily Brontë's bearings within the literary tradition of Europe in general and England in particular. But even this broad conception of tradition is not quite enough, because she utilised certain elements of the folk tradition and folk culture; the patterns of belief and thought prevalent among the village folk, the oral literature of the people, and the stories and anecdotes circulating among them. All these are skilfully woven into the structure of *Wuthering Heights* and they account for its peculiar flavour and uncanny atmosphere.

Mr. Brontë, it may be noted, was a great gossip and teller of tales whenever it pleased him. He used to enliven the breakfast table with stories of his parishioners. Gerin in her biography of Emily informs us further that Ellen Nussey "hearing and observing the hilarious effect of his racy tales on the children, while she herself was shocked by them, had to admit that it was to such sources that *Wuthering Heights* owed its being". Lest we misconstrue this assertion to mean that Emily's novel is untouched by literary influences, let us remind ourselves that *Wuthering Heights* is a preparation of many ingredients drawn from literary and folk traditions.

As to the form and narrative scheme of the novel, they are also not new in absolute terms. Creative use of the journal mode, first person narrative, servant narrator — all these devices had been employed in earlier literature. In Maria Edgeworth's *Castle Rackrent*, the story is related by the Steward, Thady Quirk. And if Henry Fielding's view that a novel is a comic epic in prose was known, anyone could think of beginning his story *in medias res*, as Milton had so illustriously done. Emily went a step further by taking up the story at a point near the end and what is remarkable in this bold departure is that she secured a *tour de force*.

This account of the sources that went into the making of *Wuthering Heights* shows that Emily Brontë had much deeper and extensive roots in the tradition than Jane Austen and many other novelists of the earlier period. One thing more: she not only cut across the boundaries of the genres but also went beyond the literary tradition to pick out bits and pieces from the culture of the village folk; the traditional patterns of belief, superstition and communal behaviour.

Wuthering Heights, therefore, requires us to take an inclusive view of tradition; that is to say, the cultural tradition of Europe of which the British literary tradition is a part. We have to think of the European tradition in the context of this novel because it deals mainly with a segment of the English society which had retained many links with the medieval age when culturally speaking England was a part of Europe.

Talking of liteary and folk cultures, we have come very close to a sociological theory which studies social change in developing societies in terms of Great and Little traditions – 'Great' as we shall see presently does not have the signification accorded to it by F.R. Leavis, who, in all probability, was unaware of the sociological use.

The sociological view has some relevance to the question of tradition relating to *Wuthering Heights*.

The historical fact to be taken note of first is that the rural society with its culture as pictured in *Wuthering Heights* was on the verge of mighty social changes knocking at the door. The arrival of Lockwood and the transformation brought about in the personality of Heathcliff after a few years' stay in some city are intimations of the urban ways and values, specially the modern maxims: 'business is business' and 'money is power'; Linton Heathcliff is also a product of urban upbringing. The theory of Great and Little traditions is therefore applicable to the society of *Wuthering Heights*.

The sociologist, of course, thinks of tradition as comprising both cultural and social structure. According to him the social structure of changing civilisations operates at two levels, the first, that of folks and peasants and the second, that of the elite or the 'reflective few'. The distinctive cultural patterns of the lower segment constitute the Little tradition and those of the elite form the Great tradition. In the present exposition, we are dealing only with a part of the culture, namely, literature, but in literature too the division between Great and Little traditions can be observed.

Let us not forget that the Little tradition, in the field of literature is rich with songs, lullabies, tales, anecdotes, proverbs, sayings, and a lot more literary material which has stood the test of time; all this literature is largely oral and exists in a number of versions. The medieval ballads which were collected and printed in the eighteenth and nineteenth centuries are, properly speaking, a part of the Little tradition, although they are now included in the Great tradition.

By now, the drift of this seeming digression might have been guessed: it was intended to bring home the fact that Emily Brontë exploited, unlike Jane Austen and many other novelists, both the Great and the Little traditions of Europe and in this regard she is in the company of such great writers as Homer and Shakespeare. And the all inclusive tradition which Homer and Shakespeare adorn alone has the right to be called the Great tradition.

So far, we have been examining what Emily took from the tradition, her deep roots in the past literature; we shall now turn our attention to what she gave to the tradition: that which makes *Wuthering Heights* a landmark in British literature. A short, and perhaps the best, answer would be that she contributed her individual talent. With the help of her powerful imagination, she threw the elements of her reading and experience into a crucible and fashioned an artistic object new in theme, feeling and form: something in which the possibilities of the earlier masterpieces were actuated towards realisation. The earlier works of fiction stood repositioned and redefined after *Wuthering Heights* was added to the literary corpus. It threw light backwards and forwards. It modified and extended the tradition instead of making a zero contribution of a slavish imitator, and blazed the path for the future writers. The traditionality and newness of *Wuthering Heights* can very well be judged in terms of this statement by Eliot:

> The existing monuments form an ideal order among themselves, which is modified by the introduction of the new (the really new) work of art among them. The existing order is complete before the new work arrives; for order to persist after the supervention of novelty, the whole existing order must be, if ever so slightly, altered; and so the relations, proportions, values of each work of art towards the whole are readjusted; and this is conformity between the old and the new. Whoever has approved this idea of order, of the form of European, of English literature will not find it preposterous that the past should be altered by the present as much as the present is directed by the past.
>
> ("Tradition and the Individual Talent")

Literary tradition in its subjective aspect represents a community's aesthetic awareness in its quality, scope and depth; and in its sublime moments and great works it strives to become the music of humanity, rising to the universal through the particular. The tradition in this form accommodating such other factors as artistry, thought, and moral vision, can certainly provide the critic with better and more balanced standards for evaluating a work than those prescribed by F.R. Leavis. We shall, therefore, reconsider the issue of greatness in the light of this new insight.

14. A Great Work

When John Canning sat down to select one hundred great books as the editor of a compilation of introductory articles, he had to answer the question: what is a great book?

> I used three principles in determining my selection: first, outstanding literary merit; second, the most highly original thinking in various branches of knowledge; third, deep spiritual insight. Here and there, rarely, a work reaches the highest standard in two of these categories; and, even more rarely, in all three. But most are pre-eminent examples of one or other of these divisions.
>
> (*One Hundred Great Books*)

A glance through the foregoing pages (or any commentary by a competent critic) preceded, of course, by a close reading of the text, or only the latter, will in all probability, convince any sensitive and fair-minded reader that *Wuthering Heights* clearly satisfies two of the three criteria to a fairly high degree, if not the highest. No wonder that *Wuthering Heights* is one of the literary works selected. Equally relevant is the single, but highly meaningful, attribute mentioned by Lawrence Durrell in his Introduction to Cannings's book:

> If one had to provide a short list of books which have, in their various ways moulded the cultural sensibility of Europe and the world one could hardly improve upon this guide.

Wuthering Heights has, beyond doubt, moulded the cultural sensibility of Europe and the world and continues to do so. In the present age, when industrialism has taken a complete hold of man (Heathcliff was both a victim and beneficiary of industrialism), the problem of evil in its causation, growth and effect has assumed a new urgency, since evil in the modern age can no longer be separated from 'the business mentality'; the other form of evil, namely a reincarnation of primitive violence and cruelty, as manifested by Hindley and Heathcliff, is equally a matter for deep concern; and yet, there is something deep down us which will tenanciously continue to long for the eventual overthrow of evil by the forces of youthful beauty and love and the dreamers of mankind, like Emily Brontë in the closing chapters of her book, will not fail humanity in its moments of need.

A SHORT BIBLIOGRAPHY

I. Original Works

Wuthering Heights (1847) by Ellis Bell (pseudonym)

—., Second Edition (1850) with an "Editor's Preface" by Currer Bell (Charlotte Brontë)

—., With an "Introduction" by Bonamy Dobree and "Biographical Notice of Ellis and Acton Bell" along with "Editor's Preface" both by Charlotte Brontë (Delhi: Indus, 1992).

—., With an "Introduction" by H.W. Garrod (O.U.P., 1930).

—., With an "Introduction" by Mark Schorer (New York: Rhinehart, 1960).

The Complete Poems of Emily Jane Bronte ed. C.W. Hatfield (New York, 1941).

II. Biography

Gerin, Winifred. *Emily Brontë: A Biography* (London: OUP 1971).

III. Critical Books and Chapters in Books

Cecil, David. "Emily Brontë and *Wuthering Heights*" in *Early Victorian Novelists* (Delhi: Kalyani Publishers, Indian edition, 1972).

De Laar, Elisabeth, Th. M. Van *The Inner Structure of Wuthering Heights* (The Hague: Mouton, 1969).

Drew, Elizabeth, "Emily Brontë: *Wuthering Heights*" in *The Novel* (New York: Dell Publishing Co., 1963).

Dry, F.S., *The Sources of Wuthering Heights* (1937).

Eagleton, Terry, *Myths of Power: A Marxist Study of the Brontës* (London: MacMillan, 1975).

Everitt, Alastair (ed.), "*Wuthering Heights*": *An Anthology of Criticism* (London, 1967).

Kavanagh, C.S., *Symbolism of "Wuthering Heights"* (London, 1920).

Kettle Arnold, "Emily Brontë : *Wuthering Heights*" in *English Novel I* (Delhi: B.I. Publication, Indian edition, 1978).

Petit, J.P. (ed.), *Emily Brontë* (Penguinë, 1973).

Read, Herbert, "Charlotte and Emily Brontë" in *Essays in Literary Criticism* (London: Faber, 1969).

Sanger, C.P., *The Structure of Wuthering Heights* (London, 1926 repr. 1968).

Traversi, Derek, "The Brontë Sisters and *Wuthering Heights*' in *From Dickens to Hardy*. Edited by Boris Ford (Penguin, 1982).

Willy, Margaret, *Brontë: Wuthering Heights*" (London: MacMillan 1966).

Woolf, Virginia, *Jane Eyre* and *Wuthering Heights*" in *The Common Reader*, First Series (London: Hogarth Press, 1925).

IV. Articles in Periodicals

Ford, Boris, "Wuthering Heights" *Scrutiny*, VII, 4 (March, 1939).

Klingopulos, G.D., "The Novel as a Dramatic Poem II: *Wuthering Heights*". *Scrutiny*, XIV, 4 (Sept. 1947).

Viswananthan, Jacqueline, "Point of View and Unreliability in Emily Brontë's *Wuthering Heights*, Conrad's *Under Western Eyes* and Mann's *Doktor Faustus*". *Orbis Litterarum*, 29 (1974).

V. Brontë Society Publications

The Transactions of Brontë Society (Haworth, since 1895).

APPENDICES

Appendix A

Biographical Note by Charlotte Brontë (In the edition of 1850)

It has been thought that all the works published under the names of Currer, Ellis, and Acton Bell, were, in reality, the production of one person. This mistake I endeavoured to rectify by a few words of disclaimer prefixed to the third edition of *Jane Eyre*. These, too, it appears, failed to gain general credence, and now, on the occasion of a reprint of *Wuthering Heights* and *Agnes Grey*, I am advised distinctly to state how the case really stands.

Indeed, I feel myself that it is time the obscurity attending those two names – Ellis and Acton – was done away. The little mystery, which formerly yielded some harmless pleasure, has lost its interest; circumstances are changed. It becomes, then, my duty to explain briefly the origin and authorship of the books written by Currer, Ellis, and Acton Bell.

About five years ago, my two sisters and myself, after a somewhat prolonged period of separation, found ourselves reunited, and at home. Resident in a remote district where education had made little progress, and where, consequently, there was no inducement to seek social intercourse beyond our own domestic circle, we were wholly dependent on ourselves and each other, on books and study, for the enjoyments and occupations of life. The highest stimulus, as well as the liveliest pleasure we had known from childhood upwards, lay in attempts at literary composition; formerly we used to show each other what we wrote, but of late years this habit of communication and consultation had been discontinued; hence it ensued, that we were mutually ignorant of the progress we might respectively have made.

One day, in the autumn of 1845, I accidentally lighted on a Ms. Volume of verse in my sister Emily's handwriting. Of course, I was not surprised, knowing that she could and did write verse: I looked it over, and something more than surprise seized me, – a deep conviction that these were not common effusions, nor at all like the poetry women generally write. I thought them condensed and terse, vigorous and genuine. To my ear, they had also a peculiar music – wild, melancholy, and elevating.

My sister Emily was not a person of demonstrative character, nor one, on the recesses of whose mind and feelings, even those nearest and dearest to her could, with impunity, intrude unlicensed; it took hours to reconcile her to the discovery I had made, and days to persuade her that such poems merited publication. I knew, however, that a mind like hers could not be without some latent spark of honourable ambition, and refused to be discouraged in my attempts to fan that spark to flame.

Meantime, my younger sister quietly produced some of her own compositions, intimating that since Emily's had given me pleasure, I might like to look at hers. I could not but be a partial judge, yet I thought that these verses too had a sweet sincere pathos of their own.

We had very early cherished the dream of one day becoming authors. This dream, never relinquished even when distance divided and absorbing tasks occupied us, now suddenly acquired strength and consistency: it took the character of a resolve. We agreed to arrange a small selection of our poems, and, if possible, get them printed. Averse to personal publicity, we veiled our own names under those of Currer, Ellis, and Acton Bell; the ambiguous choice being dictated by a sort of conscientious scruple at assuming Christian names positively masculine, while we did not like to declare ourselves women, because – without at that time suspecting that our mode of writing and thinking was not what is called 'feminine' – we had a vague impression that authoresses are liable to be looked on with prejudice; we had noticed how critics sometimes use for their chastisement the weapon of personality, and for their reward, a flattery, which is not true praise.

The bringing out of our little book was hard work. As was to be expected, neither we nor our poems were at all wanted; but for this we had been prepared at the outset; though inexperienced ourselves, we had read the experience of others. The great puzzle lay in the difficulty of getting answers of any kind from the publishers to whom we applied. Being greatly harassed by this obstacle, I ventured to apply to the Messrs. Chambers, of Edinburgh, for a word of advice; *they* may have forgotten the circumstance, but I have not, for from them I received a brief and business-like, but civil and sensible reply, on which we acted, and at last made a way.

The book was printed: it is scarcely known, and all of it that merits to be known are the poems of Ellis Bell. The fixed conviction I held, and hold, of the worth of these poems has not indeed received the confirmation of much favourable criticism; but I must retain it notwithstanding.

Ill-success failed to crush us: the mere effort to succeed had given a wonderful zest to existence; it must be pursued. We each set to work on a prose tale: Ellis Bell produced *Wuthering Heights*, Acton Bell, *Agnes Grey*, and Currer Bell also wrote a narrative in one volume. These Mss. were perseveringly obtruded upon various publishers for the space of a year and a half; usually, their fate was an ignominious and abrupt dismissal.

At last *Wuthering Heights* and *Agnes Grey* were accepted on terms somewhat impoverishing to the two authors; Currer Bell's book found acceptance nowhere, nor any acknowledgment of merit, so that something like the chill of despair began to invade his heart. As a forlorn hope, he tried one publishing house more – Messrs. Smith and Elder. Ere long, in a much shorter space than that on which experience had taught him to calculate – there came a letter, which he opened in the dreary expectation of finding two hard hopeless lines, intimating that Messrs. Smith and Elder 'were not disposed to publish the Ms.,' and, instead, he took out of the envelope a letter of two pages. He read it trembling. It declined, indeed, to publish that tale, for business reasons, but it discussed its merits and demerits so courteously, so considerately, in a spirit so rational, with a discrimination so enlightened, that this very refusal cheered the author better han a vulgarly-expressed acceptance would have done. It was added, that a work in three volumes would meet with careful attention.

I was then just completing *Jane Eyre*, at which I had been working while the one volume tale was plodding its weary round in London: in three weeks I sent it off; friendly and skilful hands took it in. This was in the commencement of September 1847; it came out before the close of October following, while *Wuthering Heights* and *Agnes Grey*, my sisters' works, which had already been in the press for months, still lingered under a different management.

They appeared at last. Critics failed to do them justice. The immature but very real powers revealed in *Wuthering Heights* were scarcely recognized; its import and nature were misunderstood; the identity of its author was misrepresented; it was said that this was an earlier and ruder attempt of the same pen which had produced *Jane*

Eyre. Unjust and grievous error! We laughed at it at first, but I deeply lament it now. Hence, I fear, arose a prejudice against the book. That writer who could attempt to palm off an inferior and immature production under cover of one successful effort, must indeed be unduly eager after the secondary and sordid result of authorship, and pitiably indifferent to its true and honourable meed. If reviewers and the public truly believed this, no wonder that they looked darkly on the cheat.

Yet I must not be understood to make these things subject for reproach or complaint; I dare not do so; respect for my sister's memory forbids me. By her any such querulous manifestation would have been regarded as an unworthy, and offensive weakness.

It is my duty, as well as my pleasure, to acknowledge one exception to the general rule of criticism. One writer, endowed with the keen vision and fine sympathies of genius, has discerned the real nature of Wuthering Heights, and has, with equal accuracy, noted its beauties and touched on its faults*. Too often do reviewers remind us of the mob of Astrologers, Chaldeans, and Soothsayers gathered before the 'writing on the wall,' and unable to read the characters or make known the interpretation. We have a right to rejoice when a true seer comes at last, some man in whom is an excellent spirit, to whom have been given light, wisdom, and understanding; who can accurately read the 'Mene, Mene, Tekel, Upharsin' of an original mind (however unripe, however inefficiently cultured and partially expanded that mind may be); and who can say with confidence, 'This is the interpretation thereof.'

Yet even the writer to whom I allude shares the mistake about the authorship, and does me the injustice to suppose that there was equivoque in my former rejection of this honour (as an honour, I regard it). May I assure him that I would scorn in this and in every case to deal in equivoque; I believe language to have been given us to make our meaning clear, and not to wrap it in dishonest doubt.

The Tenant of Wildfell Hall by Acton Bell, had likewise an unfavourable reception. At this I cannot wonder. The choice of subject was an entire mistake. Nothing less congruous with the writer's nature could be conceived. The motives which dictated this choice were pure, but, I think, slightly morbid. She had, in the course of her life, been called on to contemplate, near at hand and for a long

---

* See the Palladium for September 1850. [The article is known to be by Sidney Dobell.]

time, the terrible effects of talents misused and faculties abused; hers was naturally a sensitive, reserved, and dejected nature; what she saw sank very deeply into her mind; it did her harm. She brooded over it till she believed it to be a duty to reproduce every detail (of course with fictitious characters, incidents, and situations) as a warning to others. She hated her work, but would pursue it. When reasoned with on the subject, she regarded such reasonings as a temptation to self-indulgence. She must be honest; she must not varnish, soften, or conceal. This well-meant resolution brought on her misconstruction and some abuse, which she bore, as it was her custom to bear whatever was unpleasant, with mild, steady patience. She was a very sincere and practical Christian, but the tinge of religious melancholy communicated a sad shade to her brief, blameless life.

Neither Ellis nor Acton allowed herself for one moment to sink under want of encouragement; energy nerved the one, and endurance upheld the other. They were both prepared to try again; I would fain think that hope and the sense of power was yet strong within them. But a great change approached: affliction came in that shape which to anticipate is dread; to look back on, grief. In the very heat and burden of the day, the labourers failed over their work.

My sister Emily first declined. The details of her illness are deep-branded in my memory, but to dwell on them, either in thought or narrative, is not in my power. Never in all her life had she lingered over any task that lay before her, and she did not linger now. She sank rapidly. She made haste to leave us. Yet, while physically she perished, mentally, she grew stronger than we had yet known her. Day by day, when I saw with what a front she met suffering, I looked on her with an anguish of wonder and love. I have seen nothing like it; but, indeed, I have never seen her parallel in anything. *Stronger than a man, simpler than a child, her nature stood alone.* The awful point was, that, while full of ruth for others, on herself she had no pity; the spirit was inexorable to the flesh; from the trembling hand, the unnerved limbs, the faded eyes, the same service was exacted as they had rendered in health. To stand by and witness this, and not dare to remonstrate, was a pain no words can render.

Two cruel months of hope and fear passed painfully by, and the day came at last when the terrors and pains of death were to be undergone by this treasure, which had grown dearer and dearer to our hearts as it wasted before our eyes. Towards the decline of that day, we had nothing left of *Emily* but her mortal remains as consumption left them. *She died December 19, 1848.*

We thought this enough: but we were utterly and presumptuously wrong. She was not buried ere Anne fell ill. She had not been committed to the grave a fortnight, before we received distinct intimation that it was necessary to prepare our minds to see the younger sister go after the elder. Accordingly, she followed in the same path with slower step, and with a patience that equalled the other's fortitude. I have said that she was religious, and it was by leaning on those Christian doctrines in which she firmly believed, that she found support through her most painful journey. I witnessed their efficacy in her latest hour and greatest trial, and must bear my testimony to the calm triumph with which they brought her through. *She died May 28, 1849.*

What more shall I say about them? I cannot and need not say much more. In externals, they were two unobtrusive women; a perfectly secluded life gave them retiring manners and habits. *In Emily's nature the extremes of vigour and simplicity seemed to meet.* Under an unsophisticated culture, inartifical tastes, and an unpretending outside, lay a secret power and fire that might have informed the brain and kindled the veins of a hero; but she had no worldly wisdom; her powers were unadapted to the practical business of life; she would fail to defend her most manifest rights, to consult her most legitimate advantage. An interpreter ought always to have stood between her and the world. Her will was not very flexible, and it generally opposed her interest. *Her temper was magnanimous, but warm and sudden; her spirit altogether unbending.*

Anne's character was milder and more subdued; she wanted the power, the fire, the originality of her sister, but was well-endowed with quiet virtues of her own. Long-suffering, self-denying, reflective, and intelligent, a constitutional reserve and taciturnity placed and kept her in the shade, and covered her mind, and especially her feelings, with a sort of nun-like veil, which was rarely lifted. *Neither Emily nor Anne was learned; they had no thought of filling their pitchers at the well-spring of other minds*; they always wrote from the impulse of nature, the dictates of intuition, and from such stores of observation as their limited experience had enabled them to amass. I may sum up all by saying, that for strangers they were nothing, for superficial observers less than nothing; but for those who had known them all their lives in the intimacy of close relationship, they were genuinely good and truly great.

This notice has been written, because I felt it a sacred duty to wipe the dust off their gravestones, and leave their dear names free from soil.

September 19, 1850 Currer Bell

Appendix B

Charlotte Brontë's Preface to the Edition of 1850

I have just read over *Wuthering Heights*, and, for the first time, have obtained a clear glimpse of what are termed (and, perhaps, really are) its faults; have gained a definite notion of how it appears to other people – *to strangers who knew nothing of the author; who are unacquainted with the locality where the scenes of the story are laid; to whom the inhabitants, the customs, the natural characteristics of the outlying hills and hamlets in the West-Riding of Yorkshire are things alien and unfamiliar.*

To all such Wuthering Heights must appear a rude and strange production. The wild moors of the north of England can for them have no interest; the language, the manners, the very dwellings and household customs of the scattered inhabitants of those districts, must be to such readers in a great measure unintelligible, and – where intelligible – repulsive. Men and women who, perhaps, naturally very calm, and with feelings moderate in degree, and little marked in kind, have been trained from their cradle to observe the utmost evenness of manner and guardedness of language, will hardly know what to make of the rough, strong utterance, the harshly manifested passions, the unbridled aversions, and headlong partialities of unlettered moorland hinds and rugged moorland squires, who have grown up untaught and unchecked, except by mentors as harsh as themselves. *A large class of readers, likewise, will suffer greatly from the introduction into the pages of this work of words printed with all their letters, which it has become the custom to represent by the initial and final letter only – a blank line filling the interval. I may as well say at once that, for this circumstance, it is out of my power to apologize; deeming it, myself, a rational plan to write words at full length.* The practice of hinting by single letters those expletives with which profane and violent people are wont to garnish their discourse, strikes me as a proceeding which, however well meant, is weak and futile. I cannot tell what good it does – what feeling it spares – what horror it conceals.

With regard to the rusticity of Wuthering Heights, I admit the charge, for I feel the quality. It is rustic all through. It is moorish, and wild, and knotty as the root of health. Nor was it natural that it should be otherwise; the author being herself a native and nursling of the moors. Doubtless, had her lot been cast in a town, her writings, if she had written at all, would have possessed another character. Even had chance or taste led her to choose a similar subject, she would have treated it otherwise. Had Ellis Bell been a lady or a gentleman accustomed to what is called 'the world,' her view of a remote and unreclaimed region, as well as of the dwellers therein, would have differed greatly from that actually taken by the homebred country girl. Doubtless it would have been wider – more comprhensive; whether it would have been more original or more truthful is not so certain. As far as the scenery and locality are concerned, it could scarcely have been so sympathetic: Ellis Bell did not describe as one whose eye and taste along found pleasure in the prospect; *her native hills were far more to her than a spectacle; they were what she lived in, and by, as much as the wild birds, their tenants, or as the heather, their produce*. Her descriptions, then, of natural scenery, are what they should be, and all they should be.

Where delineation of human character is concerned, the case is different. I am bound to avow that she had scarcely more practical knowledge of the peasantry amongst whom she lived, than a nun has of the country people who sometimes pass her convent gates. My sister's disposition was not naturally gregarious; circumstances favoured and fostered her tendency to seclusion; except to go to church or take a walk on the hills, she rarely crossed the threshold of home. Though her feeling for the people round was benevolent, intercourse with them she never sought; nor, with very few exceptions, ever experienced. And yet she knew them: knew their ways, their language, their family histories; she could hear of them with interest, and talk of them with detail, minute, graphic, and accurate; but *with* them she rarely exchanged a word. Hence it ensued that what her mind had gathered of the real concerning them, was too exclusively confined to those tragic and terrible traits of which, in listening to the secret annals of every rude vicinage, the memory is sometimes compelled to receive the impress. *Her imagination, which was a spirit more sombre than sunny, more powerful than sportive, found in such traits material whence it wrought creations like Heathcliff, like Earnshaw, like Catherine. Having formed these beings, she did not know what she had done. If the auditor of her work, when read in manuscript, shuddered under the grinding influence of natures so relentless and implacable, of spirits so lost and fallen; if it was complained that the mere hearing of certain vivid and fearful scenes banished sleep by night, and disturbed mental peace by day, Ellis Bell would wonder what was meant, and suspect the complainant of affectation.* Had she but lived, her mind would of itself have grown like a strong tree, loftier, straighter, wider-spreading, and its matured fruits would have attained a mellower ripeness and sunnier bloom; but on that mind time and experience alone could work: to the influence of other intellects, it was not amenable.

Having avowed that over much of *Wuthering Heights* there broods 'a horror of great darkness'; that, in its storm-heated and electrical atmosphere, we seem at times to breathe lightning, let me point to those spots where clouded daylight and the eclipsed sun still attest their existence. For a specimen of true benevolence and homely fidelity, look at the character of Nelly Dean; for an example of constancy and tenderness, remark that of Edgar Linton. (*Some people will think these qualities do not shine so well incarnate in a man as they would do in a woman, but Ellis Bell could never be brought to comprehend this notion: nothing moved her more than any insinuation that the faithfulness and clemency, the long-suffering and loving-kindness which are esteemed virtues in the daughters of Eve, become foibles in the sons of Adam. She held that mercy and forgiveness are the divinest attributes of the Great Being who made both man and woman, and that what clothes the Godhead in glory, can disgrace no form of feeble humanity*). There is a dry saturnine humour in the delineation of old *Joseph*, and some glimpses of grace and gaiety animate the *younger Catherine*. Nor is even the first heroine of the name destitute of a certain strange beauty in her fierceness, or of honesty in the midst of perverted passion and passionate perversity.

Heathcliff, indeed, stands unredeemed; never once swerving in his arrow-straight course to perdition, from the time when 'the little black-haired, swarthy thing, as dark as if it came from the Devil,' was first unrolled out of the bundle and set on its feet in the farm-house kitchen, to the hour when Nelly Dean found the grim, stalwart corpse laid on its back in the panel-enclosed bed, with wide-gazing eyes that seemed 'to sneer at her attempt to close them, and parted lips and sharp white teeth that sneered too'.

Heathcliff betrays one solitary human feeling, and that *is not* his love for Catherine; which is a sentiment fierce and inhuman: a passion such as might boil and glow in the bad essence of some evil genius; a fire that might form the tormented centre – the ever-suffering soul of a magnate of the infernal world: and by its quenchless and ceaseless ravage effect the execution of the decree which dooms him to carry Hell with him wherever he wanders. *No; the single link that connects Heathcliff with humanity is his rudely confessed regard for Hareton Earnshaw – the young man whom he has ruined; and then his half-implied esteem for Nelly Dean. These solitary traits omitted, we should say he was child neither of Lascar nor gipsy, but a man's shape animated by demon life – a Choul – an Afreet.*

Whether it is right or advisable to create beings like Heathcliff, I do not know: I scarcely think it is. But this I know; the writer who possesses the creative gift owns something of which he is not always master – something that at times strangely wills and works for itself. He may lay down rules and devise principles, and to rules and principles it will perhaps for years lie in subjection; and then, haply without any warning of revolt, there comes a time when it will no longer consent to 'harrow the valleys, or be bound with a band in the furrow' – when it 'laughs at the multitude of the city, and regards not the crying of the driver' – when, refusing absolutely to make ropes out of sea-sand any longer, it sets to work on statue-hewing, and you have a Pluto or a Jove, a Tisiphone or a Psyche, a Mermaid or a Madonna, as Fate or Inspiration direct. Be the work grim or glorious, dread or divine, you have little choice left but quiescent adoption. As for you – the norminal artist – your share in it has been to work passively under dictates you neither delivered nor could question – that would not be uttered at your prayer, nor suppressed nor changed at your caprice. If the result be attractive, the World will praise you, who little deserve praise; if it be repulsive, the same World will blame you, who almost as little deserve blame.

Wuthering Heights was hewn in a wild workshop, with simple tools out of homely materials. The statuary found a granite block on a solitary moor: gazing thereon, he saw how from the crag might be elicited a head, savage, swart, sinister; a form moulded with at least one element of grandeur – power. He wrought with a rude chisel, and from no model but the vision of his meditations. With time and labour, the crag took human shape; and there it stands colossal, dark, and frowning, half statue, half rock: in the former sense, terrible and goblin-like; in the latter, almost beautiful, for its colouring is of mellow grey, and moorland moss clothes it; and heath, with its blooming bells and balmy fragrance, grows faithfully close to the giant's foot.

Currer Bell

Appendix C

Some Poems of Emily Brontë

REMEMBRANCE

Cold in the earth – and the deep snow piled above thee,
    Far, far removed, cold in the dreary grave!
Have I forgot, my only Love, to love thee,
    Severed at last by Time's all-severing wave?

Now, when alone, do my thoughts no longer hover
    Over the mountains, on that northern shore,
Resting their wings where heath and fern-leaves cover
Thy noble heart for ever, ever more?

Cold in the earth – and fifteen wild Decembers
    From those brown hills have melted into spring:
Faithful, indeed, is the spirit that remembers
    After such years of change and suffering!

Sweet Love of youth, forgive, if I forget thee,
    While the world's tide is bearing me along;
Other desires and other hopes beset me,
    Hopes which obscure, but cannot do thee wrong!

No later light has lightened up my heaven,
    No second morn has ever shone for me;
All my life's bliss from thy dear life was given,
    All my life's bliss in the grave with thee.

But, when the days of golden dreams had perished,
    And even Despair was powerless to destroy;
Then did I learn how existence could be cherished,
    Strengthened and fed without the aid of joy.

Then did I check the tears of useless passion –
    Weaned my young soul from yearning after time;
Sternly denied its burning wish to hasten
    Down to that tomb already more than mine.

And, even yet, I dare not let it languish,
Dare not indulge in memory's rapturous pain;
Once drinking deep of that divinest anguish,
How could I seek the empty world again?

THE OLD STOIC

Riches I hold in light esteem,
And Love I laugh to scorn;
And lust of fame was but a dream,
That vanished with the morn:

And if I pray, the only prayer
That moves my lips for me
Is, 'Leave the heart that now I bear,
And give me liberty!'

Yes, as my swift days near their goal,
'Tis all that I implore;
In life and death a chainless soul,
With courage to endure.

MY LADY'S GRAVE

The linnet in the rocky dells,
The moor-lark in the air,
The bee among the heather bells
That hide my lady fair:

The wild deer browse above her breast;
The wild birds raise their brood;
And they, her smiles of love caressed,
Have left her solitude!

I ween that when the grave's dark wall
Did first her form retain,
They thought their hearts could ne'er recall
The light of joy again.

They thought the tide of grief would flow
Unchecked through future years;
But where is all their anguish now,
And where are all their tears?

Well, let them fight for honour's breath,
    Or pleasure's shade pursue –
The dweller in the land of death
    Is changed and careless too.

And, if their eyes should watch and weep
    Till sorrow's source were dry,
She would not, in her tranquil sleep,
    Return a single sigh!

Blow, west wind, by the lonely mound,
    And murmur, summer streams –
There is no need of other sound
    To soothe my lady's dreams.

LAST LINES

    No coward soul is mine,
No trembler in the world's storm-troubled sphere:
    I see Heaven's glories shine,
And faith shines equal, arming me from fear.

    O God within my breast,
Almighty, ever-present Deity!
    Life – that in me has rest,
As I – undying Life – have power in Thee!

    Vain are the thousand creeds
That move men's hearts: unutterably vain;
    Worthless as withered weeds,
Or idlest froth amid the boundless main,

    To waken doubt in one
Holding so fast by Thine infinity;
    So surely anchored on
The steadfast rock of immortality.

    With wide-embracing love
Thy spirit animates eternal years,
    Pervades and broods above,
Changes, sustains, dissolves, creates, and rears.

    Though earth and man were gone,
And suns and universes ceased to be,

And Thou were left alone,
Every existence would exist in Thee.

There is not room for Death,
Nor atom that his might could render void:
Thou – Thou art Being and Breath,
And what Thou art may never be destroyed.

A DEATH SCENE

'O Day! he cannot die
When thou so fair art shining!
O Sun, in such a glorious sky,
So tranquilly declining;
'He cannot leave thee now,
While fresh west winds are blowing,
And all around his youthful brow
Thy cheerful light is glowing!

'Edward, awake, awake –
The golden evening gleams
Warm and bright on Arden's lake –
Arouse thee from thy dreams!

'Beside thee, on my knee,
My dearest friend, I pray
That thou, to cross the eternal sea,
Wouldst yet one hour delay:

'I hear its billows roar –
I see them foaming high;
But no glimpse of a further shore
Has blest my straining eye.

'Believe not what they urge
Of Eden isles beyond;
Turn back, from that tempestuous surge,
To thy own native land.

'It is not death, but pain
That struggles in thy breast–
Nay, rally, Edward, rouse again;
I cannot let thee rest!'

One long look, that sore reproved me
For the woe I could not bear –
One mute look of suffering moved me
To repent my useless prayer:

And, with sudden check, the heaving
Of distraction passed away;
Not a sign of further grieving
Stirred my soul that awful day.

Paled, at length, the sweet sun setting;
Sunk to peace the twilight breeze:
Summer dews fell softly, wetting
Glen, and glade, and silent trees.

Then his eyes began to weary,
Weighed beneath a mortal sleep;
And their orbs grew strangely dreary,
Clouded, even as they would weep.

But they wept not, but they changed not,
Never moved, and never closed;
Troubled still, and still they ranged not –
Wandered not, nor yet reposed!

So I knew that he was dying –
Stooped, and raised his languid head;
Felt no breath, and heard no sighing,
So I knew that he was dead.

THE PRISONER

A FRAGMENT

In the dungeon-crypts idly did I stray,
Reckless of the lives wasting there away;
'Draw the ponderous bars! open, Warder stern!'
He dared not say me nay – the hinges harshly turn.

'Our guests are darkly lodged,' I whispered, gazing through
The vault, whose grated eye showed heaven more grey than blue;
(This was when glad Spring laughed in awaking pride;)

'Aye, darkly lodged enough!' returned my sullen guide.
Then, God forgive my youth; forgive my careless tongue;
I scoffed, as the chill chains on the damp flagstones rung:
'Confined in triple walls, art thou so much to fear,
That we must bind thee down and clench thy fetters
here?'

The captive raised her face; it was as soft and mild
As sculptured marble saint, or slumbering unweaned
child;
It was so soft and mild, it was so sweet and fair,
Pain could not trace a line, nor grief a shadow there!

The captive raised her hand and pressed it to her brow;
'I have been struck,' she said, 'and I am suffering now;
Yet these are little worth, your bolts and irons strong;
And, were they forged in steel, they could not hold me
long.'

Hoarse laughed the jailor grim: 'Shall I be won to hear;
Dost think, fond, dreaming wretch, that I shall grant thy
prayer?
Or, better still, wilt melt my master's heart with groans?
Ah! sooner might the sun thaw down these granite
stones.
'My master's voice is low, his aspect bland and kind,
But hard as hardest flint the soul that lurks behind;
And I am rough and rude, yet not more rough to see
Than is the hidden ghost that has its home in me.'
About her lips there played a smile of almost scorn.
'My friend', she gently said, 'you have not heard me
mourn;
When you my kindred's lives, *my* lost life, can restore,
Then may I weep and sue, – but never, friend, before!
'Still, let my tyrants know, I am not doomed to wear
Year after year in gloom, and desolate despair;
A messenger of Hope comes every night to me,
And offers for short life, eternal liberty.
'He comes with western winds, with evening's wandering
airs,
With that clear dusk of heaven that brings the thickest
stars.

Winds take a pensive tone, and stars a tender fire,
And visions rise, and change, that kill me with desire.
'Desire for nothing known in my maturer years,
When joy grew mad with awe, at counting future tears.
When, if my spirit's sky was full of flashes warm,
I knew not whence they came, from sun or thunder-storm.
'But, first, a hush of peace – a soundless calm descends;
The struggle of distress, and fierce impatience ends;
Mute music soothes my breast – unuttered harmony,
That I could never dream, till Earth was lost to me.
'Then dawns the Invisible; the Unseen its truth reveals;
My outward sense is gone, my inward essence feels:
Its wings are almost free – its home, its harbour found,
Measuring the gulf, it stoops and dares the final bound.
'Oh! dreadful is the check – intense the agony –
When the ear begins to hear, and the eye begins to see;
When the pulse begins to throb, the brain to think again;
The soul to feel the flesh, and the flesh to feel the chain.
'Yet I would lose no sting, would wish no torture less;
The more that anguish racks, the earlier it will bless;
And robed in fires of hell, or bright with heavenly shine,
If it but herald death, the vision is divine!'
She ceased to speak, and we, unanswering, turned to go –
We had no further power to work the captive woe:
Her cheek, her gleaming eye, declared that man had given
A sentence, unapproved, and overruled by Heaven.

THE STANZAS

Often rebuked, yet always back returning
To those first feelings that were born with me,
And leaving busy chase of wealth and learning
For idle dreams of things which cannot be:

Today, I will seek not the shadowy region;
Its unsustaining vastness waxes drear;
And visions rising, legion after legion,
Bring the unreal world too strangely near.

I'll walk, but not in old heroic traces,
  And not in paths of high morality,
And not among the half-distinguished faces,
  The clouded forms of long-past history.

I'll walk where my own nature would be leading
  It vexes me to choose another guide –
Where the grey flocks in ferny glens are feeding,
  Where the wild wind blows on the mountainside.

What have those lonely mountains worth revealing?
  More glory and more grief than I can tell:
The earth that wakes one human heart to feeling
  Can centre both the worlds of Heaven and Hell.

*